James Edward Murdoch, Thomas Buchanan Read, George Henry
Boker

## Patriotism in Poetry and Prose

Being Selected Passages from Lectures and Patriotic Readings

James Edward Murdoch, Thomas Buchanan Read, George Henry Boker

**Patriotism in Poetry and Prose**
*Being Selected Passages from Lectures and Patriotic Readings*

ISBN/EAN: 9783337420208

Printed in Europe, USA, Canada, Australia, Japan

Cover: Foto ©Thomas Meinert / pixelio.de

More available books at **www.hansebooks.com**

# PATRIOTISM

IN

# POETRY AND PROSE:

BEING

𝕾𝖊𝖑𝖊𝖈𝖙𝖊𝖉 𝕻𝖆𝖘𝖘𝖆𝖌𝖊𝖘

FROM LECTURES AND PATRIOTIC READINGS

BY

## JAMES E. MURDOCH.

ALSO,

## POEMS

BY

THOMAS BUCHANAN READ, GEORGE H. BOKER,
FRANCIS DE HAES JANVIER,

AND OTHER AMERICAN AUTHORS,

COMMEMORATIVE OF THE

GALLANT DEEDS OF OUR NOBLE DEFENDERS ON LAND AND SEA.

PHILADELPHIA:

J. B. LIPPINCOTT & CO.

1865.

To MESSRS. JAMES L. CLAGHORN,

FERDINAND J. DREER,

AND JOSEPH HARRISON, JR.

GENTLEMEN:—Accept my thanks for the generous sympathy in my efforts to serve this cause which has induced you to undertake the publication of this little book, the proceeds of which are to be applied to the wants of our sick and wounded soldiers.

Your devotion to our country's cause, your untiring efforts in and your generous contributions to the glorious work of sustaining and comforting such of our noble defenders as stand in need of the Good Samaritan's office,—these good deeds expressed in your individual services are but the types of the noble virtues and generous sympathies of the loyal citizens of Philadelphia, which find an echo in the heart of every Union-loving member of the Great Republic.

I regret that my continued illness compels me to abandon my original intentions in the publication of the book. And yet I feel assured that it will meet at your hands, and from the favor of the public, attention and appreciation which its merits could not venture to call forth,—that is, at least, as far as my humble contributions to its pages are concerned.

May God bless the efforts of our loyal countrymen to alleviate the suffering and sorrows of those who are fighting for

3

our Government! and may His merciful providence restore peace to the land, and the land to the supremacy of law and order, under that sacred emblem of Liberty and Union, the dear "Old Flag"!

Truly, your friend and obedient servant,

JAMES E. MURDOCH.

PHILADELPHIA, May 19, 1864.

TO THE

MOTHERS AND WIVES, SISTERS AND DAUGHTERS,

OF

The Brave Men

WHO HAVE STOOD AS A LIVING WALL

BETWEEN

THE NATIONAL UNITY AND HONOR, AND THE ASSAULTS OF ARMED REBELS,

*THIS VOLUME IS DEDICATED*

BY

JAMES E. MURDOCH,

WHO, IN EXPRESSING HIS VENERATION FOR THE PATRIOTIC SERVICES CONFERRED ON THEIR COUNTRY, IN ITS HOUR OF TRIAL AND SUFFERING, BY THE LOYAL WOMEN OF AMERICA, CALLS TO HIS AID THE FOLLOWING BEAUTIFUL LINES.

# The Brave at Home.

(Extract from "The Wagoner of the Alleghanies.")

BY T. BUCHANAN READ.

The maid who binds her warrior's sash,
  With smile that well her pain dissembles,
The while beneath her drooping lash
  One starry tear-drop hangs and trembles,
Though Heaven alone records the tear,
  And fame shall never know the story,
Her heart has shed a drop as dear
  As e'er bedew'd the field of glory.

The wife who girds her husband's sword,
  Mid little ones who weep or wonder,
And bravely speaks the cheering word,
  What though her heart be rent asunder,
Doom'd nightly in her dreams to hear
  The bolts of death around him rattle,
Hath shed as sacred blood as e'er
  Was pour'd upon a field of battle!

The mother who conceals her grief,
  While to her breast her son she presses,
Then breathes a few brave words and brief,
  Kissing the patriot brow she blesses,
With no one but her secret God
  To know the pain that weighs upon her,
Sheds holy blood as e'er the sod
  Received on Freedom's field of honor!

# PREFACE.

It would be unjust to introduce this volume to the reader without some mention of the public services of the patriotic gentleman to whom it owes its origin. With Mr. Murdoch's "Readings" we are all familiar. In the lecture-room, the hospital, the camp, and under the falling shells of the enemy, he has raised his eloquent voice, since the beginning of our great national contest, with an effect that will not soon be forgotten by his numerous auditors. He has stimulated the patriotism of our citizens, he has comforted the sufferings of our wounded, and he has inflamed the courage of our soldiers. The pecuniary returns from his Readings have been applied in all cases, and without any deduction for his personal expenses or professional labor, to aid in alleviating the condition of the sick and the wounded. In this way he has collected and handed over to the proper disbursing agents not only thousands, but tens of thousands, of dollars,—no trifling contribution to be earned and distributed through the exertions of one man, whose health was not always robust, and who was frequently obliged to pause in his noble work and recruit his strength, wasted by the very energy of his charitable labors.

Without entering into details, we shall give a brief narrative of Mr. Murdoch's services to the cause of his country. He is disposed to consider his efforts as humble and of small public importance, when viewed in the light of the tremendous

events which are daily passing before our eyes, and to wish
that Heaven had gifted him with higher attributes and a wider
field of action, in order that his achievements might be com-
mensurate with his desires. We shall not quarrel with Mr.
Murdoch's estimate of himself. Modesty is too rare and too
beautiful a quality to be drawn from its seclusion by open
criticism. Whatever may have been the value of his labors,
they have been earnest, single in their purpose, entirely unselfish, and perfectly successful within the limits of their
sphere. Mr. Murdoch does not claim to be either a poet or an
orator: yet he has set before us the most beautiful thoughts of
the former with a passion, an energy, and a skilful modulation
of voice that have seldom been rivalled by the latter. We are
perfectly content with the scope of his work. He fills a place
that would have been vacant without him; and although, since
he began his peculiar career, he has raised around him a
crowd of imitators, none has equalled him in merit or ap-
proached him in usefulness.

During the popular excitement which followed the firing
upon the flag of Sumter, Mr. Murdoch was on his way from
Milwaukie to fulfil a professional engagement at Pittsburg.
He could not be insensible to the spirit which was rising
around him, and which increased in enthusiasm at every step
of his journey. The President's first call for volunteers was
arriving at every telegraphic station, and the spark which bore
the message seemed to have kindled a flame in every heart.
On arriving at Pittsburg, Mr. Murdoch was met by the intelli-
gence that his younger son, Thomas Forrest Murdoch, had
enlisted in a Zouave regiment and was then on his way to
Washington. Although on that night Mr. Murdoch was adver-
tised to play "Hamlet," he threw up his engagement and

started in search of his brave son. At Lancaster he found his boy in the ranks, patiently awaiting the order to move forward, and resolved to persevere in the course which he had chosen. What could the father do but confirm his son's choice and bestow a blessing upon him? Touched with the natural action, the comrades of his son, with a true American impulse, called upon Mr. Murdoch for a speech. The speech was made to them; and in that speech the orator not only animated the regiment, but he also convinced himself as to the line of duty which he was called upon to pursue. He at once abandoned his theatrical career, resolving to devote all his time, talent, and energy to the cause of his country, and not to reappear upon the stage until that cause should be triumphant. Mr. Murdoch made this great pecuniary sacrifice from no distaste to his profession. Like all other professions, he regards it as an honorable one when honorably followed; and at the close of the war it is his intention to return to a vocation in which he, at least, has always enjoyed the respect and admiration of his countrymen. He has adhered to the resolution thus formed most manfully, although tempted on all sides by the managers of theatres with offers of engagements that would have been far more remunerative to him than any which he had previously accepted, and although his failing health has again and again warned him to abandon his arduous, patriotic duties, and, if activity has become a necessity of his nature, to return to the lighter labors of his former profession.

The sacrifice of his professional career has not been the only one which Mr. Murdoch has made for his country. The noble boy with whom he parted in Lancaster is now lying beneath the bloody sod of the battle-field of Chickamauga. Captain Thomas Forrest Murdoch received his first commission as lieu-

tenant for his gallantry in the campaign which closed with
the terrible battle of Shiloh. At the battle of Stone River he
served upon the staff of General Van Cleve; his horse was
shot under him; and for his brave conduct upon that occasion
he was promoted to a captaincy. He fell at the head of General Van Cleve's line of battle in the first day's fight at Chickamauga, shouting to the men, "Come on, boys! try them once
more!" Memorable words, the spirit of which his country
adopted in its subsequent struggles. "Try them again!" has
been, and shall continue to be, our motto, until the dying war-
cry of the gallant young soldier shall be drowned in the over-
whelming shout of triumph.

Mr. Murdoch's elder son, Captain James E. Murdoch, found
it impossible to remain quietly at home, with the news of battle
ringing in his ears and seeming to reproach him for his back-
wardness. He therefore shouldered his musket and followed
his brother to the field. He was promoted for good conduct
soon after he joined the army, in which he served on the
staff of Brigadier-General Sill until that distinguished man
fell gloriously at the battle of Stone River. Captain James E.
Murdoch led his company through the long and bloody actions
at Chickamauga, although his physical condition scarcely
warranted his bravery; and at the close of the second day's
fight but a handful of men answered to the roll-call of the
company, which originally represented one hundred of the
brave farmer-boys of his father's immediate neighborhood,
Warren county, Ohio. Captain James E. Murdoch was afterwards obliged to quit active military duty, on account of his
physical disability. He retired, with an honorable record and
the highest recommendations from his corps and division commanders, and obtained a position in the invalid service. He

has since, however, returned to civil life, to cheer, as we hope, his father's declining years.

Mr. Murdoch himself has also seen some active service in the ranks of his country. At the call of the Governor of Ohio, he sallied out with the volunteers when the rebels threatened Cincinnati. He acted as aid to Commodore Duble in the gunboat flotilla on the Ohio River, and he afterwards served on the staff of that gallant soldier and loyal Kentuckian, Major-General Lovel Rousseau. For these services, as for his more peaceful efforts, Mr. Murdoch never received, nor desired to receive, a cent of pay from the Government.

When Mr. Murdoch came to the East, during the present spring, it was with the intention of continuing his course of "Readings," of visiting the Army of the Potomac, and inspiring the soldiers with the enthusiasm which his recitations have always created in the Army of the Cumberland, and of collecting the money and publishing the volume which he intended to devote to the "Relic Fund." He has failed to carry out a part of his plan, through the incapacity produced by many and, at times, serious attacks of illness. This volume is the result of so much labor as he has been able to perform; and the editor asks for it the indulgence which is usually accorded to a work produced under unfavorable circumstances and amidst the distractions of private suffering and unparalleled public excitement.

Various sums of money have been received as subscriptions to the Ladies' Societies in aid of soldiers' families, sick and wounded soldiers, &c. A copy of the book is to be presented to each subscriber. When that demand is satisfied, the book will be offered to the public, and the proceeds, after defraying expenses, will be handed to such societies as the committee may determine, for the relief of the soldiers. Of course, no subscriptions can be received after this date. The original intention of printing the subscribers' names has been abandoned, on account of the increased size of the book, as it now contains nearly one-third more of printed matter than was at first intended. The entire profits from the publication will be given to the charities above mentioned.

# CONTENTS.

# PATRIOTISM

IN

# POETRY AND PROSE.

---

## Introduction to Patriotic Readings: delivered in the Senate-Chamber of the United States.

### (EXTRACT FROM MR. MURDOCH'S LECTURES.)

IT is my ambition to illustrate and defend the great cause in which our country is now engaged, by presenting such specimens of patriotic poetry, written by my own countrymen, and by others; as may be influential in exciting national pride, and in keeping alive that feeling, without which no nation has ever been able to defend and preserve itself.

The great and good cause for which the Administration is battling against a host of traitors and factious enemies at home and a legion of interferers abroad, aroused my deepest sympathies from the very onset, and induced me to give up the profession of the actor for the time-being, and to devote myself to such efforts as would contribute relief to the sick and wounded soldiers of the Republic. I feel assured that the offices of the good physician and surgeon can be wonderfully aided and advanced by pleasant and cheerful thoughts in the patient, which are often excited and maintained by the tone of the nurse or the sprightly comrade; and hence the home-like ditty, or the time-loved hymn, when sung by lips of hopeful sympathy, expands and secures the good effects produced by the probe and the knife, the potion and the ointment. Hence I have sought occasion to raise my voice, to give utterance to patriotic poetry and prose, together with scriptural recitations, in our hospitals and "Homes," wherever the judgment of the surgeons attending sanctioned the performance.

I know, too, what good results have been attained to the toiling and patient soldier, when he joins in, or listens to, the strains of song or hymn chanted during the long and weary march. How often have I observed, in the bivouac or at the camp-fire, after reading a poem of which the soldier's suffering and the honor of his flag have been the theme, the hitherto separate groups of officers and men mingle together, while the silent tear, and the glow of patriotic pride, spoke in eloquent terms of the presence of that generous sympathy which binds man to man, and is, indeed, the corner-stone of all nationality.

To cherish this spirit, and assist in cementing that bond of unity which should bind us together in this crisis by indissoluble bands, I have attempted, through the medium of my elocutionary and dramatic experience, to interpret, and to intensify, the glorious lyrics, poems, and ballads that have been written by our loyal bards to commemorate the noble deeds of our soldiers and sailors, and dedicated by them to that soul of heroism and self-sacrifice now so beautifully and potently expressed in the spirit and acts of the noblest army ever marshalled to save a suffering and imperilled people.

I have tendered my services to the cause of the Republic

in a spirit arising from a conviction that the citizen is bound
to make the music of the nation's war or fight to it. I
prefer to help as the trumpeter was accused of doing in
Æsop's fable. I am constrained to say that I have been
in a measure impelled to my present course from a sense
of gratitude in return for the ample remuneration of the
labors of a long professional career so generously tendered
by my fellow-citizens. I have striven by my professional
donations to prove to my countrymen that, though from
physical inability I was unable to continue in the field
during a regular campaign, I am still willing to labor that
I may help to revive and sustain the proper tone and unity
of the free and loyal States in support of our Government.

It is merely justice to myself to affirm, here, that whatever I may say or do in defence of the nation and the
Administration arises from a deep-seated conviction that
my duties as an American citizen are inseparably connected with my duties to my Maker, and that I am bound
to defend the former in order to obey the commands of the
latter,—my country first, my friends afterwards. I oppose
the enemies of my country and Government as I would
hurl back the intruder on my hearth-stone.

The man who stands at my door with the torch and the
axe, I am impelled by the promptings of self-preservation
to strike down. I acknowledge no tie of kindred and
blood under such circumstances; I strike in defence of
that which God has given me to protect,—of all that is
dear to man on earth. In the language of the law, my
house is my castle: the Government is the rock on which
my house is built; the hand that undermines the one
destroys the other. The Government is the law; the law
is the creation of the people, in their sovereign capacity as
a tribe or a nation. Therefore, that body to which the people

2*

have delegated the administration of the law becomes for the time-being part and parcel of the Government. It cannot be assailed without attacking the Constitution. The man who, under the conceded right to criticize the acts of the Government, assumes the right first to abuse it, and then to embarrass its operations, by bringing its character under reproach and destroying its influence, and, finally, opposes or incites others to oppose its decrees, becomes by such acts in the eyes of the law a traitor and a rebel, as much as he who takes up arms against the legitimate Government of his country. This would be the decision in the courts in time of peace; how much more, then, is the conduct of such men treasonous when the whole nation is in a state of war, and the Government struggling with a rebellion whose object is to dismember the country and destroy the Constitution? Every word and deed calculated to destroy the popular confidence in the power of the Government to defend itself, under such circumstances, is a blow aimed at the vitality of the nation, and a stab in the back of every soldier whose face is turned to the armed rebels who strike at him in front. The man who, covertly or openly, seeks the destruction of my country's defenders, or gives aid and encouragement to my country's foes, is a public enemy, for whom I have nothing but the bitter word and, at the proper time, the deadly blow. Those who are not for the Government are against it.

I have many and dear friends in the disloyal States, as well as disloyal friends in the loyal States, who are opposed to my course and views in the present struggle; and though I am ready to meet them in the field, North or South, to try the justice of the cause I uphold, still, from a sense of gratitude, I frankly affirm that my heart yearns towards them, and, were I swayed by my affections instead of my sense of right and wrong, I should be inclined to find excuses for their rebellious attitude.    I cannot entirely shut out of my heart and memory recollections of friendly offices and kindly sympathies extended to me, in times gone by, by those who, without doubt, were happier under the then existing state of things than they could ever be were their wildest schemes of sectional aggrandizement perfected and secured.

I can truly say, " Not that I loved Cæsar less, but that I loved Rome more," is the cause of my antagonism to the rebellious attitude of the seceding States.

---

## Poetry a Substitute for Speech-Making.

### (An Extract from Mr. Murdoch's Lectures.)

" The American Flag," by Joseph Rodman Drake, needs no prologue.    It is probably the finest lyric the world has ever known or read; and it is to be regretted that, when it is sung, it is adapted to a mere opera-air.

When Cincinnati was threatened, and I among the rest of her citizens volunteered to her defence, I was induced to recite this grand national hymn under the following circumstances.

Our pickets were skirmishing with those of the enemy; within sight of our intrenchments, our citizens of all classes and ages had been working in the rifle-pits the previous day and night, and during the morning of the day I speak of, and after partaking of their mid-day meal, they were resting from their labors, under the shade of some large beech-trees.    In passing from the head-quarters of General

A. J. Smith, to Fort Mitchell, where my duty as officer of the fatigue forces called me that day, I was hailed by a well-known voice and asked to stop and give the amateur upholders of Adam's profession something to cheer and inspirit them before resuming their labors of the afternoon. "A speech! a speech!" was the cry.

But I had no confidence in my ability to address an assemblage (in which I recognized some of our leading statesmen, judges, and lawyers) in a speech upon so momentous an occasion.

I simply remarked to them that it was a pleasant sight to see the citizens of a great republic ignoring the conventional lines which mark the intercourse of a large city, and working together, heart and hand, to resist the attack of a common enemy.

"Why not, then, my friends, throw down the old walls of partition which divide you politically, and, until this unnatural strife is ended, present one bold unflinching front to all foes of the Government and our national existence, whoever they may be and from whatever quarter they may come? Why not unite, and stand fearlessly by the Government as long as it is assailed, and thus manfully assert your determination to uphold it and preserve it, and thereby prove your love for the country, the whole country, and the glorious old flag?"

I then proceeded to recite Drake's poetic address to the American flag. At the close of the recitation, cheer upon cheer went up, that, in the language of Shakspeare,

"made the welkin ring,
And mock'd the deep-mouthed thunder."

Had the enemy attacked us at that moment, I firmly believe that band of citizens would, in the absence of muskets (for they were not armed), have hurled themselves down the hillside and manfully dealt upon the foe with their picks and spades.

A sturdy old Irishman stepped out from the crowd and tendered me his hand. "Faith,"said he, "I don't know your name, sir, but that's not the matter: 'tisn't to your name I have any thing to say, but 'tis to your speech! Arrah, my jewel, they brought us out here yesterday, and meself and some of the others were not as well pleased as we might have been at a wake or a wedding. But for meself, I will venture to say, had I heard you make that speech on the other side of the river, the son of Molly Dougherty would have come over without a jaw or a grumble; and, faith, I believe I would have been after having a good musket wid me, instead of the pickaxe and spade.

"Long life to you, sir, and to your speech about the Stars and the Stripes; for if any thing can make them better and brighter than they are, it's just the like of such talk as yourself makes over 'em. Sure, sir, we'll all work the longer and the easier because of such music as that.'

## The American Flag.

BY JOSEPH RODMAN DRAKE.

When Freedom, from her mountain height,
　Unfurl'd her standard to the air,
She tore the azure robe of night,
　And set the stars of glory there!
She mingled with its gorgeous dyes
The milky baldric of the skies,
And striped its pure celestial white
With streakings of the morning light,
Then, from his mansion in the sun,
She call'd her eagle bearer down,

And gave into his mighty hand
The symbol of her chosen land!

Majestic monarch of the cloud,
    Who rear'st aloft thy regal form,
To hear the tempest-trumpings loud,
And see the lightning lances driven,
    When strive the warriors of the storm,
And rolls the thunder-drum of heaven,—
Child of the Sun! to thee 'tis given
    To guard the banner of the free,
To hover in the sulphur smoke,
To ward away the battle-stroke,
    And bid its blendings shine afar,
    Like rainbows on the cloud of war,
        The harbingers of victory!

Flag of the brave! thy folds shall fly,
The sign of hope and triumph high!
When speaks the signal-trumpet tone,
And the long line comes gleaming on,
Ere yet the life-blood, warm and wet,
Has dimm'd the glistening bayonet,
Each soldier's eye shall brightly turn
To where thy sky-born glories burn,
And as his springing steps advance,
Catch war and vengeance from the glance.
And when the cannon-mouthings loud
Heave in wild wreaths the battle shroud,
And gory sabres rise and fall
Like shoots of flame on midnight pall,
Then shall thy meteor glances glow,
    And cowering foes shall shrink beneath
Each gallant arm that strikes below
    That lovely messenger of death.

Flag of the seas! on ocean wave
Thy stars shall glitter o'er the brave;

When death, careering on the gale,
Sweeps darkly round the bellied sail,
And frighted waves rush wildly back
Before the broadside's reeling rack,
Each dying wanderer of the sea
Shall look at once to heaven and thee,
And smile to see thy splendors fly
In triumph o'er his closing eye.

Flag of the free heart's hope and home,
  By angel-hands to valor given,
Thy stars have lit the welkin dome,
  And all thy hues were born in heaven.
Forever float that standard sheet,
  Where breathes the foe but falls before us,
With Freedom's soil beneath our feet,
  And Freedom's banner streaming o'er us!

---

## Mr. Lincoln at Home in Springfield, and Mr. Lincoln at the White House in Washington.

(EXTRACT FROM MR. MURDOCH'S LECTURES.)

WHILE in Springfield, Illinois, on professional business,
I met Mr. Lincoln in the studio of my friend Thomas
Jones, the sculptor, who was modelling Mr. Lincoln's bust
at the time; and I had quite a lengthened conversation
with the future President. This was before Mr. Lincoln had
been inaugurated. Telegrams were received in town that
morning, stating that Charleston had been burned down by
shells thrown into it by Major Anderson. The Legislature
of Illinois had not yet been organized, although the members were all present. This was a political trick, intended

to make capital for the Democratic party. The consequences were that great excitement prevailed in the city.
Mr. Lincoln remarked, in reply to my question of what he
thought of the aspect of things, and of our future :—

"Sir, it appears to me we are in the midst of a great national crisis, and under the control of circumstances evidently
fashioned by the hand of Providence to produce a mighty
revolution in the affairs of the American people, and perhaps of the entire world. But I have no fear of the result.
If we can only keep the people on the track, and prevent
scares and panics, we shall come through all right. Our
people, sir, are a very excitable body, apt to switch off on
side-tracks and at way-stations, sometimes, for the mere
novelty of the change, rather than for any determinate
object, merely because 'the lead is taken, and the cry is
up.' Now, sir, I do not think this is the sober second
thought of the people, but an impulse arising out of ex-
citability. Their political rulers know this, and they often
raise the cry of 'Elephant!' and, you know, the popular
wish to see that animal is very great. Consequently, the
public mind is fired (as our neighbors have been firing the
Southern heart); and, you know, when the pulse is quick,
the muscle is active, *and matter is moved*, while the judgment is very apt, for the time-being, 'to go out visiting,'
as your friend Mr. Weller says. [I had been reading Pick-
wick the evening before.] Now, sir, I hold in my hands,"
he continued (crumpling up several telegrams), "some of
the most mischievous matters this nation has to contend
with,—things gotten up and flashed over the country to
create *fogs* and *mists*, in order that designing men may mis-
lead their more honest neighbors. But, sir, there is a sun
whose beams scatter and dispel all such foul vapors,—the
sun of truth; and if we will only await its coming forth,—

for, no matter how beclouded it may be, it will come forth (the longer hidden the brighter it will shine), it will enlighten the vision and gladden the hearts of all who desire light and not darkness. Our way is gloomy, and it may become blacker and more murky; but, sir, the light of God's providence will make all clear yet. To be sure, we may not have a bonfire at the beginning of every day's progress, but we shall find illuminations often enough, if we will only keep steadily on the track, be cool and calm in the face of danger, and have faith in the future. We shall come out of all this seeming chaos and confusion a wiser and a better people. There is no doubt that in such a storm as that which is brewing in our country, there must be many wrecks and much suffering; much of valuable matter will have to go overboard; but enough will be saved to make a good voyage yet, and, I hope, to set the ship all right for another cruise.

"Let the men to whom are intrusted the interests of the people illuminate these truths, and think more of the nation than of themselves. Let them review their oaths of office, and consider how fearfully responsible they are for all their acts in this crisis. Thus influenced and directed, the common enemy will be beaten down, and order restored. Let the people know the facts, let them see the danger; but let every effort be made to allay public fears, to inspire the masses with confidence and hope, and, above all, to frown down every attempt to create a panic.

"Thus the public pulse will beat healthily, and we can safely judge of and contend with the disease which is developing itself in the social and political body of the nation

"There is, no doubt, sir, a great conflict for principle impending, and we must be, as our forefathers were, in the right, and success is certain. The Almighty will bring us safely

3

through this, if we only keep cool, and maintain the right patiently and fearlessly. *I have no fears* for the result, and I don't *intend* to have any, no matter how things work."

I began my conversation with Mr. Lincoln without intent or purpose. I had no sympathy with him, nor with the Republican party of that day; yet I shook his hand, impressed, at parting, with the conviction that Abraham Lincoln had a mission to perform, and that he would perform it according to his convictions of justice and duty. I had long thought that the gathering corruptions in political matters required, for their cure, treatment of a more positive and thorough character than our national doctors had been dealing in for many years past; and I now began to think that the new treatment—under the new school and practice of the President—would, although it might possibly be administered with a parable-like story or a pleasant joke, prove any thing but pleasant in its operation to some patients.

In speaking of this interview to my father, on my return to Ohio, I said,—

"I have seen the man who is, under Providence, to control and direct the crisis and the consequences in this our day of trial and tribulation. A man combining the firmness (which may lie concealed under a 'method,' but still is firmness) of General Jackson, with the amiability of Henry Clay; a man not one jot or tittle less imbued with patriotism and love of country than those great and good men were. Abraham Lincoln, if I am not mistaken in him, will disappoint two sets of men,—those who voted for him, thinking to control him in his administration, and those who voted against him, thinking he was not the man to master the situation of affairs and bring order out of chaos."

` My father was an old-line Democrat, of the Jefferson and Jackson stamp; and I shall never forget his look when saying to me, the tears choking his utterance :—

"May God grant that your impressions prove prophecies! We want an *honest man* now, and not a mere politician, to direct us. These are evil times, and evil men are at work, for evil purposes. Honesty and truth may set us right, and if Mr. Lincoln will forget party and self, and serve his God and his country, I may yet be spared the sad fate of going down to a grave dug in the soil of a bleeding and a dismembered country. O party! party! what a hydra-headed monster thou art! We must kill party-spirit, my son, or party-spirit will kill the nation."

My father died before the battle of Bull Run took place, and before that next cruel thing was done,—the cowardly pleading for peace so basely put forth by the Breckinridge wing of the Democratic party. Thank God! these two inflictions were spared the old man, who loved his country, its history, and its institutions, truly and deeply, and who could have conceived of nothing so entirely wicked as to countenance even the supposition that the United States of America could ever become the *dis*-united States; and, worse than all, that a Democrat could have been found base enough to say to those who were holding the knife at the throat of their bleeding country, "Let them alone; let them go! We know they are murderers and assassins, who have struck a deadly blow at their life-giving mother; but we may *want them in the future*. Let them alone; let them go!" `

Let any disinterested man compare the subject-matter of these remarks of Mr. Lincoln, with his course from the time he left Springfield until he arrived in Washington City, together with his suggestions and actions since. Let

them, I repeat, compare what has gone before of his acts
and deeds, with what he is doing, and they cannot fail, I
think, to acknowledge that his whole course has been consistent and honest, and so shaped as to render available
"the events and circumstances" which have arisen out of
the acts of the Catilines of the South, and the consequences
thus forced upon the Administration.

That Mr. Lincoln is a joker, we know; and that he is a
serious thinker, and an honest man, we know also. That
this same "levity" (as some white-haired sinners call it)
of Mr. Lincoln has been the "nice fence" with which he
has foiled many a well-aimed thrust made at his arguments
by his opponents, can plainly be seen by any man "who
looks through the deeds" as well as the "words of men."
The following quotation may not be inapplicable to our
subject:—

"He hath a right ready wit and a queasy mode of raillery
that to querulous questioners may not sit so nicely as might
be on shoulders somewhat bowed with dignities and honors.
But yet, beshrew me, his mirth has meaning in it, and I
would rather quarrel with than miss it.  Ah, he's a merry
man, ay, a merry and a proper; and for one like me, whose
crutch and spectacles will sometimes chide the quips and
quillets of heartier days, there can be no better gossip to
counsel, or crack a nut or joke withal, than our good
keeper of the seals and parchments."

Melchior Muhlenburg, the patriot parson of the Revolution, said,—

> "In this, the morn of Freedom's day,
> There is a time to fight and pray."*

---

* Extract from "The Wagoner of the Alleghanies," by Thomas
Buchanan Read.

Mr. Lincoln thinks, I suppose, that there is a time to joke and pray; and if, as his detractors affirm, he joked all the way to Washington, if he did not pray also (as we believe he did, and fervently, too), he at least desired the prayers of others, as the circumstances recorded in the following poem will show. It is from the pen of a lady of Philadelphia, Mrs. Anna Bache.

## Lincoln at Springfield, 1861.

*"The fear of the Lord is the beginning of wisdom."*

THERE stood a man in the West Countrie,
Slender and tall and gaunt was he;
His form was not cast in a courtier's mould,
But his eye was bright, and his bearing bold.
A crowd had gather'd to hear him speak,
And the blood surged up in his sunburn'd cheek;
Familiar with toil was his outstretch'd hand,
 For a man of the people was he,
Who had learn'd to obey, ere call'd to command.—
 Such men are the pride of the West Countrie.

"My friends,—elected by your choice,
 From the long-cherish'd home I go,
Endear'd by heaven-permitted joys,
 Sacred by heaven-permitted woe.
I go, to take the helm of state,
 While loud the waves of faction roar,
And by His aid, supremely great,
Upon whose will all tempests wait,
 I hope to steer the bark to shore.
Not since the days when Washington
To battle led our patriots on,
Have clouds so dark above us met,
Have dangers dire so close beset.

3*

And *he* had never saved the land
By deeds in human wisdom plann'd,
But that with Christian faith he sought
Guidance and blessing, where he ought.
Like him, I seek for aid divine,—
His faith, his hope, his trust, are mine.
Pray for me, friends, that God may make
    My judgment clear, my duty plain ;
For if the Lord no wardship take,
    The watchmen mount the towers in vain."

He ceased ; and many a manly breast
    Panted with strong emotion's swell,
And many a lip the sob suppress'd,
    And tears from manly eyelids fell.
And hats came off, and heads were bow'd,
    As Lincoln slowly moved away ;
And then, heart-spoken, from the crowd,
In accents earnest, clear, and loud,
    Came one brief sentence, "We *will* pray !"
                        MRS. ANNA BACHE.

Desiring that Mr. Lincoln's record may be always before
the public, we copy here his letter explaining some of his
apparent inconsistencies, as they are termed.

(EXTRACT FROM THE FRANKFORT (KENTUCKY) "COMMONWEALTH,"
APRIL 26, 1864.)

The circumstances which elicited from the President the
letter are, as we understand them, about as follows:—

The Senior of the Commonwealth, Colonel Hodges, by
invitation, accompanied Governor Bramlette, and the Honorable Archie Dixon, on their recent visit to the Executive
Mansion at Washington, where they had interviews with
the President and the Secretary of War.

At the close of the interview between President Lincoln, Governor Bramlette and Senator Dixon, the President pleasantly remarked, as the other gentlemen were about retiring, that he was apprehensive that Kentucky felt unkindly towards him, in consequence of not properly understanding the difficulties by which he was surrounded, in his efforts to put down this rebellion, and that he would explain to the gentlemen some of those difficulties, if they felt inclined to hear him. A willingness was at once manifested, and the President explained to them the difficulties which he had alluded to.

On a subsequent occasion, in a conversation with Mr. Lincoln, Colonel Hodges remarked that he was satisfied that the President was greatly misunderstood by many of the citizens of Kentucky, and that he would greatly oblige him if he would write out the remarks made to Governor Bramlette and Senator Dixon, in order that, with the President's permission, they might be published in the "Commonwealth;" that, if published, the Colonel doubted not they would remove much of the prejudice which was attempted to be created against the President in Kentucky.

The President took the matter into consideration, and, shortly after his return home, the Colonel received the following, which we would commend to the deliberate consideration of the patriotic people of Kentucky :—

"EXECUTIVE MANSION,
WASHINGTON, April 4, 1864.

"A. G. HODGES, Esq., Frankfort, Kentucky:

"MY DEAR SIR:—You ask me to put in writing the substance of what I verbally said the other day, in your presence, to Governor Bramlette and Senator Dixon. It was about as follows :—

"I am naturally anti-slavery. If slavery is not wrong, nothing is wrong. I cannot remember when I did not so think and feel. And yet I have never understood that the Presidency conferred upon me an unrestricted right to act officially upon this judgment and feeling. It was in the oath I took that I would, to the best of my ability, preserve, protect, and defend the Constitution of the United States. I could not take the office without taking the oath. Nor was it my view that I might take the oath to get power, and break the oath in using the power. I understood, too, that in ordinary civil administration this oath even forbade me to practically indulge in primary, abstract judgment on the moral question of slavery. I had publicly declared this many times and in many ways. And I aver that, to this day, I have done no official act in mere deference to my abstract judgment and feeling on slavery.

"I did understand, however, that my oath to preserve the Constitution to the best of my ability, imposed upon me the duty of preserving, by every indispensable means, that Government—that nation—of which that Constitution was the organic law. Was it possible to lose the nation and yet preserve the Constitution?

"By general law, life and limb must be protected; yet often a limb must be amputated to save a life; but a life is never wisely given to save a limb. I felt that measures otherwise unconstitutional might become lawful by becoming indispensable to the preservation of the Constitution, through the preservation of the nation. Right or wrong, I assumed this ground, and now avow it. I could not feel that to the best of my ability I had even tried to preserve the Constitution, if, to save slavery, or any minor matter, I should permit the wreck of Government, country, and Constitution altogether. When, early in the war, General Frémont attempted military emancipation, I forbade it, because I did not then think it an indispensable necessity. When, a little later, General Cameron, then Secretary of War, suggested the arming of the blacks, I objected, because I did not yet think it an indispensable necessity. When, still later, General Hunter attempted military emancipation, I again forbade it, because I did not yet think the indispensable necessity had come.

"When, in March and May and July, 1862, I made earnest and successive appeals to the border States to favor compensated emancipation, I believed the indispensable necessity for military emancipation and arming the blacks would come, unless averted by that measure. They declined the proposition; and I was, in my best judgment, driven to the alternative of either surrendering the Union, and with it the Constitution, or of laying strong hands upon the colored element. I chose the latter. In choosing it, I hoped for greater gain than loss; but of this I was not entirely confident. More than a year of trial now shows no loss by it in our foreign relations, none in our home popular sentiment, none in our white military force,— no loss by it anyhow or anywhere. On the contrary, it shows a gain of quite a hundred and thirty thousand soldiers, seamen, and laborers. These are palpable facts, about which, as facts, there can be no cavilling. We have the men, and we could not have had them without the measure.

"And now, let any Union man, who complains of the measure, test himself, by writing down in one line that he is for taking these one hundred and thirty thousand men from the Union side, and placing them where they would be but for the measure he condemns. If he cannot face his cause so stated, it is only because he cannot face the truth.

"I add a word, which was not in the verbal conversation. In telling this tale, I attempt no compliment to my own sagacity. I claim not to have controlled events, but confess plainly that events have controlled me. Now, at the end of three years' struggle, the nation's condition is not what either party or any man devised or expected. God alone can claim it. Whither it is tending seems plain. If God wills the removal of a great wrong, and wills also that we of the North, as well as you of the South, shall pay fairly for our complicity in that wrong, impartial history will find therein new causes to attest and revere the justice and goodness of God.

"Yours, truly,

"A. LINCOLN."

The following letter and poem were received on the 15th of February, 1864, and read in the Senate-Chamber, on the occasion of one of my patriotic readings for the benefit of the United States Sanitary Commission.

Previous to commencing my reading, I met the President in the private room of the Vice-President, and asked him if the sentiment of the poem met with his approval, as well as the poetry. He replied,—

"Sir, I admire the one and approve the other, entirely and heartily."

I read the poem in the course of the evening, and, judging from the applause (loud and long) bestowed on it, the audience endorsed, in every sense, the poetry and the sentiment quite as fully and feelingly as Mr. Lincoln.

"Executive Mansion,
Washington, February 15, 1864.

"My dear Sir:—The President of the United States directs me to send you the enclosed little poem, and to request that, if entirely convenient, you will please to read it at the Senate-Chamber this evening.

"I have the honor to be
"Your obedient servant,
"Jno. G. Nicolay,
"*Private Secretary.*

"James E. Murdoch, Esq."

"The following patriotic lines were written by one of the most distinguished statesmen of the United States, in answer to a lady's inquiry whether he was for peace."—Editor.

## Am I for Peace? Yes!

For the peace which rings out from the cannon's throat,
    And the suasion of shot and shell,
Till rebellion's spirit is trampled down
    To the depths of its kindred hell.

For the peace which shall follow the squadrons' tramp,
   Where the brazen trumpets bray,
And, drunk with the fury of storm and strife,
   The blood-red chargers neigh.

For the peace which shall wash out the leprous stain
   Of our slavery, foul and grim,
And shall sunder the fetters which creak and clank
   On the down-trodden dark man's limb.

I will curse him as traitor, and false of heart,
   Who would shrink from the conflict now,
And will stamp it, with blistering, burning brand,
   On his hideous, Cain-like brow.

Out! out of the way! with your spurious peace,
   Which would make us rebellion's slaves!
We will rescue our land from the traitorous grasp,
   Or cover it over with graves.

Out! out of the way! with your knavish schemes,
   You trembling and trading pack!
Crouch away in the dark, like a sneaking hound
   That its master has beaten back.

You would barter the fruit of our fathers' blood,
   And sell out the Stripes and Stars,
To purchase a place with rebellion's votes,
   Or escape from rebellion's scars.

By the widow's wail, by the mother's tears,
   By the orphans who cry for bread,
By our sons who fell, we will never yield
   Till rebellion's soul is dead.

## The Prescience of the Poet.

(EXTRACT FROM MR. MURDOCH'S LECTURES.)

THE following lines are from a poem by Thomas Buchanan Read, Esq., entitled "The New Pastoral," published about ten years ago. They derive their present interest mainly from the fact that they are singularly prophetic of events which now form the murky clouds enshrouding the whole nation in one common gloom, and of the rainbow arch of hope which will hereafter break forth and dispel the darkness in the ordered time of Him who hath said, "I make peace and create evil."

Mr. Read seems to have been impressed with the idea of awakening the enthusiasm of the people in favor of their country, by elevating them above mere party strifes, and filling them with the inspiration of a great cause.

In one of the passages, you will observe, he anticipates the time when, through the machinations of the artful and designing demagogue, this fair land may be divided and desolated by civil war, and, with surprising prescience, signalizes, and almost names, the man who, from the ranks of toil and private life, may arise to redeem the nation. Whether in this peculiar passage he had the present Chief Magistrate in view, it is not for me to say; but certainly the reader cannot fail to distinguish something like a portrait of that President who, born among the people and in his early life devoted to hard toil, may, with the blessing of divine Providence, prove to be the accepted chieftain of the deliverance of the Republic, and the perpetuation of the Union.

This extract was first read in the Hall of Representatives at Washington, on the occasion of a benefit for the sick and wounded soldiers. A large and distinguished audience was present; the extract was part of my introduction; and, as I uttered the prophecy concerning the man of the West, Mr. Lincoln entered the chamber and seated himself in a chair on the right of the Speaker's stand, near the entrance. He was not observed for some moments, but gradually his presence was acknowledged by loud applause, which finally became general, as the application of his position and services to the poet's language became apparent and general. I was not aware of his presence, till, pausing in respect to the applause, I inadvertently turned, and saw the President in the chair near to the door. He came late, and, not wishing to disturb the speaker, he had entered alone, and quietly seated himself in the vacant chair.

## Extract from The New Pastoral,

### BY THOMAS BUCHANAN READ.

Oh, to roam, like the rivers, through empires of woods,
Where the king of the eagles in majesty broods,
Or to ride the wild horse o'er the boundless domain,
And to drag the wild buffalo down to the plain,
There to chase the fleet stag, and to track the huge bear,
And to face the lithe panther at bay in his lair,
Are a joy which alone cheers the pioneer's breast,
For the only true hunting-ground lies in the West!

Leave the tears to the maiden, the fears to the child,
While the future stands beckoning afar in the wild;
For there Freedom, more fair, walks the primeval land;
Where the wild deer all court the caress of her hand,

4

There the deep forests fall, and the old shadows fly,
And the palace and temple leap into the sky.
Oh, the East holds no place where the onward can rest,
And alone there is room in the land of the West!

Let contemplation view the future scene.
Afar the woods before the vision fly,
Swift as the shadow o'er the meadow-grass
Chased by the sunshine, and a realm of farms
O'erspreads the country wide, where many a spire
Springs in the valleys, and on distant hills,—
The watch-towers of the land.   Here quiet herds
Shall crop the ample pasture, and on slopes
Doze through the summer noon.   While every beast
Which prowls, a terror to the frontier fold,
Shall only live in some remember'd tale,
Told by tradition in the lighted hall,
When the red grate usurps the wooded hearth.
Here shall the city spread its noisy streets,
And groaning steamers chafe along the wharves;
While hourly o'er the plain, with streaming plume,
Like a swift herald bringing news of peace,
The rattling train shall fly; and from the East—
E'en from the Atlantic to the new-found shores
Where far Pacific rolls, in storm or rest,
Washing his sands of gold—the arrowy track
Shall stretch its iron bond through all the land.
Then these interior plains shall be as they
Which hear the ocean roar; and Northern lakes
Shall bear their produce, and return them wealth,
And Mississippi, father of the floods,
Perform their errands to the Mexic Gulf,
And send them back the tropic bales and fruits.
Then shall the generations musing here
Dream of the troublous days before their time,
And antiquaries point the very spot
Where rose the first rude cabin, and the space

Where stood the forest chapel with its graves,
And where the earliest marriage rites were said.
Here, in the middle of the nation's arms,
Perchance the mightiest inland mart shall spring;
Here the great statesman from the ranks of toil
May rise, with judgment clear, as strong as wise,
And, with a well-directed patriot blow,
Reclinch the rivets in our union-bands,
Which tinkering knaves have striven to set ajar!
Here shall, perchance, the mighty bard be born,
With voice to sweep and thrill the nation's heart,
Like his own hand upon the corded harp.
His songs shall be as precious girths of gold,
Reaching through all the quarters of the land,
Inlaid so deep within the country's weal,
That they shall hold when heavier bands shall fail,
Eaten by rust, or broke by traitor blows.
Heaven speed his coming! He is needed now!
He wisely spake who said, "Let me but sing
The songs, and let who will enact the laws."
There are whose lips are touch'd with living fire;
In this great moment are they silent now?
Lift up your foreheads, O ye glorious few,
Exalt your laurels in the gusty air!
And, like brave heralds on a windy hill,
Let your clear voices as a bugle ring!
The wild time needs you. There are trembling hearts
To strengthen and assure; and there are tongues,
Uttering they know not what, that should be drown'd,
And babbling lips that should be fill'd with song,
Lest they breathe treason unaware. Who dares,
Like that bad angel which dismember'd heaven,
Stand forth, and, with "disunion" on his lips,
Earn endless infamy? None are so base,
Or if he lives—the world on land and sea
Hides many monsters—let his villain tongue,
In its proclaiming, struck with palsy, cleave—

Cleave to the root, as with a ten years' drought,
And rot to ashes in the traitor's throat!
And may his arm which lifts the severing sword
Be lightning-shiver'd ere it gives the blow!
And on his brow be branded these black words:
"Behold the Iscariot of his native land!"
Then drive him forth in all his impotence,—
The wide earth's exile,—an abhorred show!

O thou, my country, may the future see
Thy shape majestic stand supreme as now,
And every stain which mars thy starry robe,
In the white sun of truth be bleach'd away!
Hold thy grand posture with unswerving mien,
Firm as a statue proud of its bright form,
Whose purity would daunt the vandal hand
In fury raised to shatter! From thine eye
Let the clear light of freedom still dispread
The broad, unclouded, stationary noon!
Still with thy right hand on the fasces lean,
And with the other point the living source
Whence all thy glory comes; and where unseen,
But still all-seeing, the great patriot souls
Whose swords and wisdom left us thus enrich'd,
Look down and note how we fulfil our trust!
Still hold beneath thy fix'd and sandal'd foot
The broken sceptre and the tyrant's gyves;
And let thy stature shine above the world,
A form of terror and of loveliness!

(Published in 1850.)

## 𝕮𝖍𝖊 𝕽𝖊𝖑𝖎𝖈𝖘.

(EXTRACT FROM MR. MURDOCH'S LECTURES.)

I FIRMLY believe Abraham Lincoln, our Chief Magistrate, to be earnest, honest, and truthful, and solely bent on serving the country for the country's sake. I also believe him to be imbued with unbounded faith in the justice of our country's cause, and with a never-failing hope that the efforts of his loyal countrymen throughout the length and breadth of the land, strengthened by the mercy and grace of Almighty God, will restore peace to the people and unity to the nation. In consideration of these truths, I have prepared, and will cause to be presented to the President of the nation, a memorial emblematic of the noble virtues of the people whom he represents, and of that trust in Providence by which his public acts have ever been impelled. I desire to bring to public remembrance, by the gift I have prepared, and which will be presented to Mr. Lincoln in behalf of the loyal men and women of America, some of those great national events upon which rests the true glory of our American Republic.

Among other mementoes fondly cherished, I have in my possession a piece of the Treaty Elm of William Penn, a part of the veritable keel of the old United States frigate Alliance, and a fragment of the flag-halliards of the noble ship Cumberland, lately lost in Chesapeake Bay.

In the form of an ornamental paper-weight, I have caused to be placed together these authentic relics of three great periods of our national history,—the treaty of William Penn with the aborigines, the unfurling of the flag of our Republic in '76, and the equally heroic

4*

defence of that flag against the formidable domestic treason
with which we are now contending. This memento, though
of but little intrinsic value, is to me, and I feel assured it
will be to the President, of inestimable price, as a relic of
our country's history, and a memorial of the many noble
charities which have been established during the present
war to aid the sick and wounded soldiers and their suffering
families. The cheerful, bountiful, and laborious efforts of
these truly humane institutions, aided, and in many instances
inaugurated, by the ladies, present a grand and generous
offering of a free people to the noble army of patriots
whose stalwart arms and undaunted hearts are the bulwarks of the country. This offering was conceived and
will be tendered in a truely Christian and patriotic spirit;
and its record will forever remain to express the heart-
felt sympathy and devotion which the American women
manifest for their gallant defenders. It will ever prove
how dear to them is the cause their soldiers bleed for,
and how precious is every drop of blood shed and every
pang endured by their countrymen. The sufferings of our
army, and the sustaining sympathy of our noble country-
women, have thrown around the nation and its starry
emblem a halo of religious sanctity, an atmosphere of self-
sacrificing devotion, which will forever vindicate our
patriotism from the sneers of foreign critics, and add an
almost sacred glory to the history of republican institutions.

In order to revive in the public mind the recollections
of the past, of old times and old things, and to connect
them with the passing events of the present, I will here
introduce a few words of comment and description regarding the articles which compose the mementoes I have
prepared.

First, a piece of the elm-tree which stood on the shores
of the Delaware near the city of Philadelphia, under whose
branches William Penn made his treaty with the Indians.
The morning after the old tree had been blown down, about
fifty years ago, my father, Lieutenant Thomas Murdoch, a
resident of my native city, Philadelphia, cut a piece of
the wood to keep as a memento of the locality and the
event that had made it memorable.

Second, a piece of the wood of the keel of the old
frigate Alliance, a ship whose log-book recorded triumphs
and incidents as glorious as the achievements of any vessel
in the navies of the world.

She carried the pennant of that old sea-king, Commodore Paul Jones, and bore the first American flag that
was ever saluted in a foreign port.

My father (who, I am proud to say, commanded a volun-
teer battery in the War of 1812, and was a great venerator
of every thing connected with the history of his country)
was familiar with the story of the ship, and with the old
hulk which lay in the mud of Petty's Island, opposite the
extreme northern section of Philadelphia, for nearly half
a century. Fifteen years ago, or more, perhaps, the
remains were removed, to make way for improvements;
and my father caused the workmen to cut out pieces of
the keel, which were found to be in good preservation, to
add to his stock of relics.

Third, and last, a piece of the halliards of the flag of
the frigate Cumberland, whose gallant defence against the
iron-clad Merrimac has excited the wonder and admiration
of the world. This relic was procured from the wreck and
presented to me by Mr. George B. Coal, of Baltimore, a
short time after the conflict.

These articles are wrought into a stand on which rests a

miniature anchor with a coil of cable attached, forming an emblematical paper-weight.

The anchor, being the received emblem of faith and hope, suggested the appropriateness of the present to Mr. Lincoln.

The treaty-tree represents the colonial state of the country.

The war-ship, the struggle by which our forefathers established the present Government.

The shreds of the halliards, the foul conspiracy in the South to overthrow that Government.

The simplicity and truthfulness of the President's character, the peaceable and humble nature of his early pursuits, his manly and determined opposition to wrong, the firmness with which he took his stand at the onset of the rebellion, together with his hopeful dependence on the protecting arm of Providence, and his firm trust in the mercy and goodness of our Father in heaven,—all these traits of a just and good man, holding the helm of state in a crisis involving the happiness and safety of all, point to him as the man of the nation most fitting at this moment to possess these emblems of the noble actions of his countrymen. In order to throw around this present, so simple in itself, and yet so full of rich historic value, the charm of poetic enforcement and appreciation, I will call to my aid a poem whose sublime sentiment seems to me to be equally applicable to the country and to her honest and able Chief Magistrate, the immortal lines of our own poet and fervent advocate of truth, William Cullen Bryant:—

> " Ah, never shall the land forget
>     How gush'd the life-blood of the brave,—
>  Gush'd warm with hope and courage yet
>     Upon the soil they sought to save.

# THE RELICS.

"Soon rested they who fought; but thou,
  Who minglest in the harder strife,
For truths which men receive not now,
  Thy warfare only ends with life.

"A friendless warfare, lingering long
  Through weary day and weary year;
A wild and many-weapon'd throng
  Hangs on thy front and flank and rear.

"Yet nerve thy spirit to the proof,
  And blench not at thy chosen lot:
The timid good may stand aloof,
  The sage may frown,—but faint thou not.

"Nor heed the shaft too surely cast,
  The foul and blasting bolt of scorn;
For with thy side shall dwell, at last,
  The victory of endurance born.

Truth crush'd to earth shall rise again;
  The eternal years of God are hers;
But Error, wounded, writhes in pain,
  And dies among her worshippers.

"Yea, though thou liest upon the dust,
  When they who help'd thee flee in fear,
Die full of hope and manly trust,
  Like those who fell in battle here!

"Another hand thy sword shall wield,
  Another hand the standard wave,
Till from the trumpet's mouth is peal'd
  The blast of triumph o'er thy grave!"

## The Memento to Secretary Chase.

IN every stage of human progress and trial, either in an upward or downward direction, the Almighty prescience and wisdom have called forth some power or persons to master the situation, and to direct and control the means by which the event and circumstance of the period or its crisis has been advanced and perfected.

In the affairs of the Revolution our forefathers were blessed with a man and a genius by whose direction and example order was brought out of chaos, and the military elements of the struggle so combined and employed that, though baffled and delayed for a time in their operations, success eventually crowned and rewarded them.

As George Washington was the bright particular star of the struggle whose triumph gave to the world a government which is the shield and staff of all the weak and the weary of the nations of the earth, who seek its shelter and support, so Robert Morris was the polar star by whose directing influence the financial affairs of the Revolution (though storm-tossed and buffeted by the waves of adverse seas) were brought to shelter and safe harborage. The star of Washington's popular reward culminated and blazed in the meridian of his own times, and will continue to shine as long as the sacred fires shall burn on the altar of the temple of Fame.

The services of Morris, though of no less value intrinsically than those of the nation's general, were not of a character as appreciable to the masses. The eye which can see the result of a military campaign may not discern and comprehend the subtle ramifications of financial diplomacy:

therefore the people who could as a body appreciate the services of Washington when victory crowned them with success, might not, and it is to be feared were not able to, distinguish and appreciate the genius and the means by which the brave and suffering soldiers were fed and clothed, even as poorly and as scantily as it was often their sad fate to be.

Although the full measure of fame and justice was not awarded to Robert Morris in his lifetime, yet his services and sacrifices are so incorporated with the history of the Revolution, that so long as that record stands he cannot be forgotten. Future historians will regild the bright letters in which his services were first recorded,—the just tribute paid to his merits by those who knew and felt that to the genius and labors of the great financier of 1776 the nation was as largely indebted for its independence and glory as it was to the devoted bravery of its gallant defenders in the field.

History, it is said, reproduces itself. The great rebellion followed the great revolution. The financial struggle of the one is the history of the other. Old landmarks were swept away, and a new line marked out and followed. A man and a policy were developed in one crisis; a man and a policy arose in the other. The treasury ship was stranded by the pirates who deserted her in 1860, but the wreckers did not board her before a new commander came to her rescue; energy and skill soon floated and manned her; and now, in 1864, she is steadily sailing before the favoring gales of credit and success, riding the waves of that perilous ocean in safety, in whose fogs and on whose shoals and rocks she was threatened with shipwreck.

Salmon P. Chase has not only accomplished the herculean task of averting all the threatened and existing dangers by which the finances of the nation were surrounded, but he has turned peril into security. The elements of weakness in our system of banking and currency have become, under the influence of his foresight and genius, a basis of strength. Not only have the finances of the country been so managed as fully to supply the gigantic wants of the national policy (forced into operation by the insurgents and their aiders and abettors at home and abroad), but also to provide for its future requisitions, whether for the purposes of commerce or of war, no matter what the situation of affairs may be when the rebellion is crushed, or what may arise from the maintenance of the "Monroe doctrine" in the future. To the bold, though consistent, experiments and plans of our patriotic and energetic Secretary of the Treasury do we owe "the sinews of war," by which the Government has been enabled to protect and defend itself against one of the most wicked and powerful conspiracies ever planned to destroy a nation.

Mr. Chase may be truly said to possess that inestimable jewel, embodied in the following ancient aphorism :—"The greatest honor a citizen can achieve is to deserve well of the republic." Actuated by a sincere desire to stimulate the public appreciation of such services, I have prepared a "paper-weight" of the wood of the "treaty elm" and of the Alliance; to which I have added a specimen of gold quartz procured by me from a mine in California in 1853. This memento is to be presented to Mr. Chase in the same spirit, and in behalf of the same public benefactions, as those which represent the gift to the President.

The wood of the "treaty elm" may serve to represent the peaceable character of American institutions. The wood of the old frigate will serve to symbolize the material of the nation's defences and the boundless capacity and power of the people's commerce; for the old Alliance was first a war-ship, and afterwards a merchantman. The gold quartz represents the mineral resources of the republic. The combination of these materials in the " paper-weight," and the uses to which it is adapted, may not inaptly typify the strength and wealth of the national power and resources, and illustrate their ability when applied as a " weight" to secure the national currency from the winds of factious party at home, or from the gales of envy and detraction blowing from abroad.

These " relics " will be of additional value to the recipients, as they have been the means of calling forth a generous endorsement from the lovers of the Union, in the form of subscriptions to the funds of the several institutions devoted to the soldier's wants.

At the close of the Philadelphia Sanitary Fair, the directors of that institution will forward the " weights" to Washington, and cause them to be appropriately presented to the distinguished gentlemen for whom they are designed.

---

## Items concerning the Treaty Elm.

THE following interesting facts, compiled from the best authorities, will serve to refresh our historic recollections without going into extensive reviews.

In the summer of 1682, a small vessel, called the " Welcome," sailed from England with William Penn and a company of Quakers for the shores of Delaware Bay and river,—on the borders of which lay a broad domain granted to Penn by Charles the Second.

Penn arrived, proceeded up the river to Shackamaxon,

now Kensington, and there, under the wide-spreading, but then leafless, branches of an elm-tree on the banks of the Delaware, he purchased the good will of the tribes by kind and gentle words and gifts, to them, of great value.

"We meet," said the man of peace, "in the broad pathway of good faith and good will. No advantage shall be taken on either side, but all shall be openness and love. I will not call you children, for parents sometimes chide their children too severely; nor brothers, for brothers differ. The friendship between you and me I will not compare to a chain, for that the rains might rust and the falling tree break: we are the same as if one man's body were to be divided into two parts; we are all one flesh and blood."

This plain talk, and the truthful spirit that prompted it, impressed the Indian favorably; and he replied, "We will live in love with William Penn and his children as long as the sun and moon shall endure." The Quaker kept his simply proffered faith, and the Indian dwelt in his. Voltaire says, "Penn began by making a league with his American neighbors. It is the only treaty between those nations and the Christians which was never sworn to and never broken."

Thus was established the Commonwealth of Pennsylvania, whose principles are expressed in the name of its chief city, Philadelphia, which is brotherly love.

> "Thou'lt find, said the Quaker, in me and mine
> But friends and brothers to thee and thine,
> Who abuse no power, and admit no line
>    Twixt the red man and the white.
> And bright was the spot where the Quaker came,
> To leave his hat, his drab, and his name,
> That will sweetly sound from the trump of Fame,
>    Till its final blast shall die."

The treaty-tree, as the great elm was ever afterwards called, became an object of veneration. It was blown down during a storm on the night of March 3, 1810. Its consecutive rings proved it to have been two hundred and eighty years old. The trunk was twenty-four feet in circumference. Many valuable articles for preservation were made from the wood. A monument was erected by the Penn Society upon the spot where the old tree had stood so long. The venerable Judge Peters, the esteemed and personal friend of Washington, thus wrote after the elm had fallen :—

> "Let each take a relic from that hallow'd tree,
> Which, like Penn whom it shaded, immortal shall be.
> As the pride of our forests, let elms be renown'd
> For the justly prized virtues with which they abound.
> Though time has devoted our tree to decay,
> The sage lessons it witness'd survive to this day.
> May our trustworthy statesmen, when call'd to the helm,
> Ne'er forget the wise treaty held under the elm."

The following are the inscriptions of the monument. North side, "Treaty-ground of William Penn and the Indian nation, 1682. Unbroken Faith." South side, "William Penn, born 1644, died 1718." West side, "Placed by Penn Society, Anno Domini 1827, to mark the site of the great Elm-tree." East side, "Pennsylvania founded, 1681, by deeds of peace."

## Incidents in the History of the Old War-Ship the Alliance.

THE Alliance was built at Salisbury, Massachusetts,—a place that figured as a building-station even in the seventeenth century. She was launched about the time the treaty was made with France, and named after that event. Cooper says, " She was the favorite ship of the American navy; and it may be said of the American people, during the War of the Revolution, filled some such place in the public mind as has since been occupied by her more celebrated successor the Constitution. She was a beautiful and an exceedingly fast ship, but was rendered less efficient than she might have proved, by the mistake of placing her under the command of a Frenchman, who had entered our service. This was evidently done to pay a compliment to the new allies of the Republic. This unfortunate selection produced mutinies, much discontent among the officers, and, in the end, grave irregularities. Landais was at last supposed to be insane, and was dismissed the navy."

The first prominent service this ship was employed in was to carry that gallant and devoted friend of the nation, Lafayette, to France. Then, under the command of Commodore Barry, one of the most brave and distinguished officers of the navy, she made another trip to France, carrying out Colonel Laurens as a commissioner to the French court. During the voyage back, Commodore Barry engaged two British ships of war, and in the midst of the fight, under every disadvantage, the Commodore was struck in the shoulder by a grape-shot, and carried below. One of his officers, following, stated to him the shattered condition of the ship, loss of men, &c., and asked if the colors should be struck.

"No," said the suffering Barry: "if you cannot fight the enemy, carry me on deck, and I will."

When the sailors heard the heroic answer of their commander, they rent the air with their shouts, crying that they would stick to the Commodore to the last. The fight was renewed, and the enemy's two ships struck to the Stars and Stripes.

Without enumerating further conflicts in which the Alliance maintained the honor of the flag of the young Republic, we will quote again from Cooper:—

"The peace of 1783 found the finances of the Government altogether unequal to the support of a navy. Most of the public cruisers had fallen into the hands of the enemy, or had been destroyed, and the few that remained were sold.

"The Alliance, which appears to have been a favorite ship of the service to the very last, was reluctantly parted with; but, a survey being held on her, she was disposed of, in preference to encountering the expense of repairs."

The last mention I find of the venerable pioneer of the sea is the following :—

In 1787, as an Indiaman, the Alliance frigate made a voyage to Canton, under the command of Captain Read, formerly of the navy. She still maintained her reputation for fast sailing, and was a pioneer to the last; for it will be remembered this was only two years after the opening of the China trade, she being perhaps the second or third ship of any size engaged in the traffic. My father used to speak of her in connection with the coffee-trade to Java, and with many other facts not to be found in print.

There are few instances in the navies of the world of a

ship of war achieving so many battle triumphs, and accomplishing so many peaceable missions, as this our old-time warrior.   But ships, like men, must yield to the wear and tear of time and action.

Towards the close of her career she was frequently repaired, and, being found at last unseaworthy, was condemned and broken up for her copper and iron, old junk, &c.   The hulk was run up on Petty's Island, where for many years it basked in the sunshine or braved the storm; and many a brave fellow, looking at the wreck, wiped away, perchance, a tear, with the sleeve of his coat, muttering to himself, "Perhaps that will be Jack's fate one of these days," and turning the quid in his mouth, with "Well, she was pluck to the last; and here goes for another cruise."   So saying, it may be, he lowered his tarpaulin to the Stars and Stripes, and became once more one of Uncle Sam's men.

The Constitution frigate, the ship whose glorious record took up, as it were, in 1800, the link dropped in our chain of naval history in 1783, was saved from the fate of the Alliance by Dr. Oliver Wendell Holmes, whose poem of "Old Ironsides" caused our countrymen to pause, and reconsider their intention of breaking up the nation's favorite.   This poem, one of the talented author's earliest productions, seems to me to be so apposite in this connection that I will take the liberty of making the verse speak for itself.

### Old Ironsides.

Ay, tear her tatter'd ensign down !
Long has it waved on high,
And many an eye has danced to see
That banner in the sky;

Beneath it rung the battle shout
And burst the cannon's roar:
The meteor of the ocean air
Shall sweep the clouds no more.

Her deck, once red with hero's blood,
Where knelt the vanquish'd foe,
When winds were hurrying o'er the flood
And waves were white below,
No more shall feel the victor's tread,
Or know the conquer'd knee:
The harpies of the shore shall pluck
The eagle of the sea!

Oh, better that her shatter'd hulk
Should sink beneath the wave!—
Her thunders shook the mighty deep,
And there should be her grave.
Nail to the mast her holy flag,
Set every threadbare sail,
And give her to the god of storms,
The lightning, and the gale!

---

# The Shreds of the Flag-Halliards of the Cumberland.

WE now turn to an event whose sudden and astounding results caused the European rulers to pause in their survey of maps and charts, of diagrams, budgets, and estimates, the artisans and workmen to stand and listen while the iron cooled upon the anvil, and generals and admirals, bewildered and confounded, to see their former plans of strategy and their magazines of material vanishing into thin air.

On a bright Sunday morning, in Chesapeake Bay, the

roll of drums is heard, and cannon belch forth their thunders. Then a pause, followed by the jar of iron, the crashing of timbers, the rushing of waters, the shriek and the yell of drowning men, mingling with the rattle of musketry and the roar of tremendous guns; and, behold! the pride of our ship-yard, the stately Cumberland, flashing forth her defiant death-notes even beneath the surging billows, is slowly plunging through the waters of the bay to find a resting-place on the sandy bottom.

But where is the rebel foe? Dimly seen through the battle-shroud floats the iron monster, exulting in its new-born power, and seeking another victim. But now appears upon the scene an object whose dark and moving outlines are more inexplicable still.

Swift as when the sword-fish strikes the huge leviathan of the deep, are its movements. Darting through the startled waters, it lunges its prow of iron against the armored sides of its wondering foe. Fires flash from out its bowels, bolts of steel hurtle in the air. The smoke rolls up, and, lo! the dark and wallowing monster whose grinding beak of polished metal had swept the walls of wood from its pathway, is now painfully toiling, wounded and disabled, towards the shelter of less dangerous waters.

The iron Merrimac had met her match. Desperate craft had been met by deliberate art. Labor and science and mechanical skill triumphed, and laid their trophies at the feet of their guardians and protectors,—the enterprising spirits of the North, whose genius first encouraged and developed artistic invention and willing toil, and blazoned on its banners the forge and the foundry, the lathe and the workshop.

In the same hour, republican valor vindicated the honor and integrity of free institutions, and taught the Old World that North America had the nerve and the means, the science, the muscle and the might, to maintain the position she has assumed as the standard-bearer of human progress on the Western Continent.

The determined spirit of the defence made by the Cumberland is fully illustrated in the following incident.

As the ship careened, the waves poured through her shattered side, soon overflowing the deck. In this position, the men, knee-deep in water, fired the last broadside, which, as the guns were depressed by the position of the deck, poured out their shot beneath the gushing billows; while her brave defenders, their defiant shouts mingling with the sullen roar of the cannon, their old flag flying at the peak, sank to a glorious death, leaving to their traitorous foes a damning record, that shall flush the cheek of rebellion's posterity with eternal shame.

Such deeds are the embodiment of the nation's glory. This is the sublime spirit of noble enthusiasm and patriotic devotion which shuns no danger, counts no loss, but sternly and steadfastly faces the foe wherever found in attitude to strike.

The "Don't give up the ship!" of 1812 has found its echo, and now thunders forth, in these the ever-memorable days of the Republic. That legacy of our fathers, that same unflinching spirit, shines out in the obstinate and fiery courage of our soldiers and sailors in the present struggle against treason. The ever-to-be-United States of America may challenge the annals of the ancient and the modern past, to produce more soul-stirring examples of patriotic sacrifice at the shrine of national honor than these which our loyal defenders in the field have inscribed on the roll of fame. While the glorious achievements of Farragut, Dupont, Foote, Porter, and a host of other gallant spirits, tell in tones of thunder that American sailors will brook no attempt to tarnish our glory, or to tear one star from the bright galaxy that floats·at the mast-head of the good ship "The Union." Woe! woe! to the fratricidal traitors who are leagued against our flag! Shame, eternal shame and discomfiture to all who encourage or protect them in their thrice-accursed treason! The intent and meaning of the war the North is waging, is written in unmistakable characters; and the sooner the rebels, and their aiders and abettors at home and their sympathizers abroad, read and learn, the sooner will the peace of America be restored and that of Europe secured.

# Three Eras.

## INSCRIBED TO PRESIDENT LINCOLN.

### BY THOMAS BUCHANAN READ.

Some relics, consisting of a piece of Penn's "Treaty Elm," of the old frigate "Alliance," and the halliards of the sloop-of-war "Cumberland," wrought into appropriate form, were presented to President Lincoln by James E. Murdoch, Esq.; and this poem was written to accompany them.

## The Treaty Elm.

ERE to the honor'd patriot's mansion yonder
　These charm'd and emblematic relics pass,
Upon the sacred fragments let me ponder,
While Fancy, to the admiring eye of Wonder,
　Withdraws the veil, as in a magian's glass.

I see the "Treaty Elm," and hear the rustle
　Of autumn leaves, where come the dusky troops
In painted robes and plumes, to crowd and jostle,—
A savage scene, save that the peace-apostle
　Stands central, and controls the untamed groups.

These are the boughs the forest eagle lit on,
　Long ere he perch'd upon our nation's banner;
Beneath their shade I see the gentle Briton,
And hear the contract, binding, though unwritten,
　And worded in the plain old scriptural manner.

Across the Delaware the sound comes faintly,
　And fainter still across the tide of time,
Though history yet repeats the language quaintly
That fell from lips of Penn, the calm and saintly,
　Speaking of love, the only true sublime.

This is his mission, and his sole vocation.
To hear of this, the savage round him presses.
How sweetly falls the beautiful oration
Which bids them bear the marvellous revelation
Of Christian peace through all their wildernesses!

Not to defraud them of their broad possessions
He comes, or to control their eagle pinions,
But to pledge friendship and its sweet relations,
Truth and forbearance, gentleness and patience,
To all the people of their wild dominions.

"We meet," he said, "upon the open highway
Of broad good will, and honest faith and duty.
Let love fraternal brighten every by-way,
And peace inviolate be thy way as my way,
Till all the forest blossoms with new beauty."

So spake their friend, and they revered his teaching.
They said, "We will be true to thee and thine."
And through long seasons toward their future reaching,
No act was shown their plighted faith impeaching,
Marring the compact, loving and divine.

O thou, like noble Penn, who truth adorest,
A priest at her great shrine in Freedom's temple,
While o'er this gift in thoughtful mood thou porest,
Point to the faithful children of the forest,
And bid the nations learn from their example.

## The Alliance.

HERE is an oaken relic from a bark
That speaks of olden scenes and ocean mystery,—
An anchor from the Revolution ark,
Dropt to the present through the twilight dark,
Linking the troubled periods of our history.

It may be that the sapling of this wood,
  Crown'd on the coast with vines inviting inland
Was swaying to the sea-wind's fitful mood,
Learning the rocking motion of the flood,
  When roving Norsemen stood agaze at Vinland.

Or did it feel the westward-sweeping gale—
  The wind that still of God and freedom hymneth—
Which landward drove the saintly hero's sail,
Until the sea-toss'd pilgrims, worn and pale,
  Were landed on the icy rock of Plymouth?

Where'er it grew, the woodman found the oak,
  It knew the teamster and the hewer's trestle,
It felt the hammers, snuff'd the pitchy smoke,
Then seaward, like a steed from stall, it broke,
  While Salisbury hail'd her favourite warrior vessel.

Those were the days wherein we flung defiance
  Unto a tyrant monarch and his henchmen.
We ask'd for friendship, France gave her compliance;
And hence we call'd our vessel the Alliance,
  In honor of the noble-hearted Frenchmen.

Then France was generous France: her well-earned fame
  Shed round the world a lustre of pure glory.
No Italy breathed curses on her name,
No Mexico stood pointing at her shame
  With feeble fingers, desperate and gory.

The royal vessel sought her future realm,—
  Royal, because her parent oak was regal;
And sceptred Science shaped her prow and helm,
And crowned Courage, naught could overwhelm,
  Breathed in the bosom of that fierce sea-eagle.

The ocean cormorants fled before her path.
  Her wing, descried afar, was fearful omen;

6

Full oft her desolating vengeance hath,
In the great tempest of her iron wrath,
   Sent a wild shudder through the hearts of foemen.

Hers was the enviable pride to bear
   The unselfish hero's well-beloved exemplar,
A Paladin whose heart was full of prayer
For freedom's Palestine—his soul was there.
   Forever honor'd be the good knight-templar.

O Gratitude, forget not the ovations
   Due to a noble country's nobler scion.
Let Lafayette, before the gaze of nations,
Stand canonized amidst our constellations,
   Belted with starry fame, like brave Orion.

Old Europe's waters bore her graceful keel,
   And heard the rolling of her threatening thunder;
She taught the insolent buccaneer to kneel
And sue for quarter,—taught their homes to feel
   A mingled sense of due respect and wonder.

Though she a while the doubtful Landais bore,
   It was her glorious privilege to carry
The pennant of Paul Jones, the Commodore,
The pride and terror of the sea and shore,
   And his, the hardy and intrepid Barry.

And when the war was o'er, she laid aside
   The latest vestige of the past commotion,
And to the winds of Commerce, far and wide,
Shook out her sails for other realms untried,
   And brought home treasure from the farthest ocean.

There have been doubtful Landais' on our deck,—
   The deck of state,—that wellnigh brought disaster!
But thou, obedient to a nation's beck,
Didst save the flag-ship of the world from wreck,
   O noble patriot and unswerving master!

And still thou rul'st this stormy deck of state,
   With all your sea-worn councillors in communion,
Still, with your mann'd and well-tried guns in wait,
Stand by your charge, O Captain, calm and great,
   Beneath the steadfast banner of the Union!

And when the Southern buccaneer at last
   Shall strike her colors, saying, "It is over,"
Lash on the prize and raise her jury-mast,
Stop all her leaks, make all her rigging fast,
   And bring her homeward, a repentant rover.

And when anon our battle-flag is furl'd,
   If that no insolent gauntlet lies before us,
By dastard in the hour of danger hurl'd,
Then let our ship of commerce sweep the world,
   Her deck made musical with Freedom's chorus.

# The Piece of Halliard from the Flag of the Cumberland.

THIS simple cord, by unknown fingers spun,
   Holds history in every slender fibre,—
Telling more baseness in one action done,
And of more heroism, than the sun
   E'er saw upon the storied tide of Tiber.

A shred from off the halliards of our hope,
   Our battle-banner, seldom lower'd or baffled!
Did he who twined the fellow to that rope
Behold, in his imaginary scope,
   The trembling traitor on his well-earn'd scaffold?

He should have seen, methinks, the dance of death,
   The traitors' dance in this rebellious season,
While the gaunt wizards on the Southern heath,
Like the foul hags encounter'd by Macbeth,
   With hell-born charm and chant are brewing treason.

Fierce maledictions, breathed with desperate might
  By trodden nations, longing to be freemen,
Shall fall upon them with the withering blight
Of leprous pestilence that walks at night,
  Till their own hearts shall curse their reigning demon.


## The Attack.

IN Hampton Roads, the airs of March were bland,
  Peace on the deck and in the fortress sleeping,
Till in the look-out of the Cumberland,
The sailor, with his well-poised glass in hand,
  Descried the iron island downward creeping.

A sudden wonder seized on land and bay,
  And Tumult with her train was there to follow,
For still the stranger kept its seaward way,
Looking a great leviathan blowing spray,
  Seeking with steady course his ocean wallow.

And still it came, and largen'd on the sight,—
  A floating monster,—ugly and gigantic,—
In shape a wave, with long and shelving height,
As if a mighty billow, heaved at night,
  Should turn to iron in the mid-Atlantic.

Then ship and fortress gazed with anxious stare,
  Until the Cumberland's cannon, silence breaking,
Thunder'd its guardian challenge, " Who comes there?"
But, like a rock-flung echo in the air,
  The shot rebounded, no impression making.

Then roar'd a broadside:—though directed well,
  On, like a nightmare, moved the shape defiant!
The tempest of our pounding shot and shell,
Crumbled to harmless nothing, thickly fell
  From off the sounding armor of the giant!

Uncheck'd, still onward through the storm it broke,
With beak directed at the vessel's centre,—
Then through the constant cloud of sulphurous smoke
Drove, till it struck the warrior's wall of oak,
Making a gateway for the waves to enter.

Struck, and, to note the mischief done, withdrew,
And then, with all a murderer's impatience,
Rush'd on again, crushing her ribs anew,
Cleaving the noble hull wellnigh in two.
And on it sped its fiery imprecations.

Swift through the vessel swept the drowning swell,
With splash and rush and gulfy rise appalling,
While sinking cannon rung their own loud knell.
Then cried the traitor from his sulphurous cell,
"Do you surrender?" Oh, those words were galling!

How spake our captain to his comrades then?
It was a shout from out a soul of splendor,
Echoed from lofty maintop, and again
Between-decks, from the lips of dying men,
"Sink, sink, boys, sink! but never say surrender!"

Down went the ship! Down—down—but never down
Her sacred flag to insolent dictator!
Weep for the patriot heroes doom'd to drown!
Pledge to the sunken Cumberland's renown!
She sunk—thank God!—unsoil'd by foot of traitor!

## The Apostrophe.

GREAT ruler, these are simple gifts to bring thee,—
Thee,—doubly great, the land's embodied will;—
And simpler still the song I fain would sing thee:—
In higher towers let greater poets ring thee
Heroic chimes on Fame's immortal hill.

A decade of the years its flight has taken,
  Since I beheld and pictured with my pen
How yet the land on ruin's brink might waken
To find her temples rudely seized and shaken
  By traitorous demons in the forms of men.

And I foresaw thy coming,—even pointed
  The region where the day would find its man
To reconstruct what treason had disjointed.
I saw thy brow by Honesty anointed,
  While Wisdom taught thee all her noblest plan.

Thy natal stars by angels' hands suspended,
  A holy trine, where Faith, and Hope, and Love,—
By these celestial guides art thou attended,
Shedding perpetual lustre, calm and splendid,
  Around thy path wherever thou dost move.

No earthly lore of any art or science
  Can fill the places of these heavenly three ;
Faith gives thy soul serene and fix'd reliance ;—
Hope to the darkest trial bids defiance ;—
  Love tempers all with her sublime decree.

'Tis fitting, then, these relics full of story,
  Telling ancestral tales of land and sea,—
Each fragment a sublime *memento mori*
Of heroes mantled in immortal glory,—
  Should be consign'd, great patriot, unto thee.

# Mr. Boker as a Dramatic Poet.

## (EXTRACT FROM MR. MURDOCH'S LECTURES.)

THE naval conflict below New Orleans—a conflict without a parallel in the world's history—has been graphically sketched by Mr. George H. Boker, of Philadelphia,—a writer who, until the rebellion broke out, had devoted himself entirely to dramatic and contemplative poetry, but who, when our flag was assailed, threw off his indifference to national subjects, and from that time to the present has been one of the most enthusiastic poets of the war. Mr. Boker's productions, in all the forms of verse, are marked by distinguished ability, which has been fully acknowledged by the best critics both in Europe and America. His dramas have met with decided success on the stage, his "Calaynos" having passed the ordeal of London criticism, and occupied the stage of one of the leading theatres in that city for sixty consecutive nights, Mr. Phelps, the acknowledged rival of Macready, performing the principal character. It affords me pleasure to say, here, that, among several original characters which I have introduced to American audiences, "Calaynos" stands foremost in the list, both in the gratification that its study and performance have afforded me, and in the remunerative applause and treasurer's returns of its audiences, in all the principal cities of the West (my favorite field of labor), and also in my native place, Philadelphia, having acted it in that city over fifty nights.

Apart from a consideration of his versification, one of the most striking features of Mr. Boker's poetry is the naturalness of his dramatic combination and progress. His argument is introduced, as it were, with a chord, but without further prelude; the action begins at once, and we follow, as the urchin follows the drum, not for the performer, but for the music: his feet keep time to the beat, distance and hours having no measure for eye or sense. So with Mr. Boker's ballads: his characters speak and act for a purpose, and that is to illustrate the story and express the sentiment. Hence we follow the music, realizing the poetic idea so feelingly and entirely that the imagination triumphs over the colder elements of our nature, and we are filled with that essence to which the fairy-creation owes its origin, and at last we awake from our dream of enjoyment to find that we have been feasting on fancies, brief but beautiful. This is the effect produced on the plastic mind by true art in dramatic action. The imagery and form of expression, however elevated or grand, becomes, by the proper exercise of true talent, so natural and unobtrusive that it fits the person it is intended to illustrate as a garment, while situation and surroundings are toned into the general coloring of life. Nothing is suffered to offend the eye as unnatural in form, nor any thing so exaggerated permitted in action as to repel sense or outrage the proprieties of probability or reason. To possess intuitively, and to employ feelingly and fearlessly, this perceptive sense of the true in nature, as well as the beautiful in art, is to be a dramatist. This faculty of story-telling and of mental portrait-painting, whose productions require neither preface nor catalogue for the reader's or hearer's enlightenment, is the perfection of the "art which conceals art," and is the foundation that underlies the whole dramatic structure, and, when combined with the wealth of ideal and intellectual beauty, is the sum and substance of dramatic power.

Ballad verse, in its effects on the emotional system, comes nearer dramatic force than either the epic or the lyric, because it is the true vehicle of narrative. It seems to be the natural offspring of the Thespian monologue. What that ancient exhibition of poetry was to the classic drama, ballads were to the sublime and heroic verse of Shakspeare, Milton, and Byron. It is a combination of the minstrel's song and legend, and the harper's chanted narrative to which he tuned the chords of his harp, when the deeds of chivalry and the devotion of the lover arose above the hum of the banquet or the din of assembled warriors. Mr. Boker's ballads are dramas in action and character; he tells a story clearly and well; he clothes his personages in fitting garb, and causes them to move gracefully and grandly to the measure of his verse.

Having proved his capability to accomplish dramatic success, he brings thereby to his narrative poems a power and a grace which enable him, through their instrumentality, to impart the glow and fervor of chivalric homage and eulogy of the olden time to the heroic circumstance and incident of this less romantic age.

## The Ballad of New Orleans.

JUST as the hour was darkest,
　　Just between night and day,
From the flag-ship shone the signal,
　　"Get the squadrons under way."

Not a sound but the tramp of sailors,
　　And the wheeling capstan's creak,
Arose from the busy vessels
　　As the anchors came apeak.

The men work'd on in silence,
  With never a shout or cheer,
Till 'twas whisper'd from bow to quarter,
  "Start forward!   All is clear."

Then groan'd the ponderous engines,
  Then flounder'd the whirling screw;
And, as ship join'd ship, the comrades
  Their lines of battle drew.

The moon through the fog was casting
  A blur of lurid light,
As the captain's latest order
  Was flash'd into the night :—

"Steam on! and, whatever fortune
  May follow the attack,
Sink with your bows all northward :
  No vessel must turn back."

It was hard, when we heard that order,
  To smother a rising shout;
For it waken'd the life within us,
  And we burn'd to give it out.

All wrapp'd in the foggy darkness,
  Brave Bailey moved ahead;
And stem after stern his gunboats
  To the starboard station led.

Next Farragut's stately flag-ship
  To port her head inclined;
And midmost, and most in danger,
  Bell's squadron closed behind.

Ah! many a prayer was murmur'd
  For the homes we ne'er might see;

And the silence and night grew dreadful
  With the thought of what must be.

For many a tall, stout fellow
  Who stood at his quarters then,
In the damp and dismal moonlight,
  Never saw the sun again.

Close down by the yellow river,
  In their oozy graves they rot;
Strange vines and strange flowers grow o'er them,
  And their far homes know them not.

But short was our time of musing;
  For the rebel forts discern'd
That the whole great fleet was moving,
  And their batteries on us turn'd.

Then Porter burst out from his mortars,
  In jets of fiery spray,
As if a volcano had open'd
  Where his leaf-clad vessels lay.

Howling, and screeching, and whizzing,
  The bomb-shells arch'd on high,
And then, like gigantic meteors,
  Dropp'd swiftly from the sky,—

Dropp'd down on the low, doom'd fortress
  A plague of iron death,
Shattering earth and granite to atoms
  With their puffs of sulphurous breath.

The whole air quaked and shudder'd
  As the great globes rose and fell,
And the blazing shores look'd awful
  As the open gates of hell.

Fort Jackson and Fort St. Philip,
  And the battery on the right,
By this time were flashing and thundering
  Out into the murky night.

Through the hulks and the cables, sunder'd
  By the bold Itasca's crew,
Went Bailey in silence, though round him
  The shells and the grape-shot flew.

No answer he made to their welcome,
  Till abeam St. Philip bore;
Then, oh! but he sent them a greeting
  In his broadsides' steady roar!

Meanwhile, the old man in the Hartford
  Had ranged to Fort Jackson's side:
What a sight! he slow'd his engines
  Till he barely stemm'd the tide.

Yes, paused in that deadly tornado
  Of case-shot and shell and ball,
Not a cable's length from the fortress,
  And he lay there, wood to wall!

Have you any notion, you landsmen,
  Who have seen a field-fight won,
Of canister, grape-shot, and shrapnel
  Hurl'd out from a ten-inch gun?

I tell you, the air is nigh solid
  With the howling iron flight;
And 'twas such a tempest blew o'er us
  Where the Hartford lay that night.

Perch'd aloft in the forward rigging,
  With his restless eyes aglow,

Sat Farragut, shouting his orders
    To the men who fought below.

And the fort's huge faces of granite
    Were splinter'd and rent in twain,
And the masses seemed slowly melting,
    Like snow in a torrid rain.

Now quicker and quicker we fired,
    Till between us and the foe
A torrent of blazing vapor
    Was leaping to and fro ;

While the fort, like a mighty cauldron,
    Was boiling with flame and smoke,
And the stone flew aloft in fragments,
    And the brick into powder broke.

So thick fell the clouds o'er the river,
    You could hardly see your hand,
When we heard from the foremast rigging
    Old Farragut's sharp command :

" Full head !   Steam across to St. Philip !
    Starboard battery, mind your aim !
Forecastle, there, shift your pivots !   Now
    Give them a taste of the same !"

St. Philip grew faint in replying,
    Its voice of thunder was drown'd.
"But, ha ! what is this ?   Back the engines !
    Back, back !   The ship is aground !"

And down the swift current came sweeping
    A raft spouting sparks and flame ;
Push'd on by an iron-clad rebel,
    Under our port side it came.

At once the good Hartford was blazing,
  Below, aloft, fore and aft.
"We are lost!"  "No, no; we are moving!"
  Away whirl'd the crackling raft.

The fire was soon quench'd.  One last broadside
  We gave to the surly fort;
For above us the rebel gunboats
  Were wheeling like devils at sport.

And into our vacant station
  Had glided a bulky form:
'Twas Craven's stout Brooklyn, demanding
  Her share of the furious storm.

We could hear the shot of St. Philip
  Ring on her armor of chain,
And the crash of her answering broadsides
  Taking and giving again.

We could hear the low growl of Craven,
  And Lowry's voice, clear and calm,
While they swept off the rebel ramparts
  As clean as your open palm.

Then, ranging close under our quarter,
  Out burst from the smoky fogs
The queen of the waves, the Varuna,
  The ship of bold Charley Boggs.

He waved his blue cap as he passed us;
  The blood of his glorious race,
Of Lawrence the hero, was burning
  Once more in a living face.

Right and left flash'd his heavy broadsides;
  Rams, gunboats,—it matter'd not;

Wherever a rebel flag floated
  Was a target for his shot.

All burning and sinking around him
  Lay five of the foe ; but he,
The victor, seem'd doom'd with the vanquish'd,
  When along dash'd gallant Lee.

And he took up the bloody conflict,
  And so well his part he bore,
That the river ran fire behind him,
  And glimmer'd from shore to shore.

But while powder would burn in a cannon,
  Till the water drown'd his deck,
Boggs pounded away with his pivots
  From his slowly-settling wreck.

I think our old captains in heaven,
  As they look'd upon those deeds,
Were proud of the flower of that navy
  Of which they planted the seeds.

Paul Jones, the knight-errant of ocean,
  Decatur, the lord of the seas,
Hull, Lawrence, and Bainbridge, and Biddle,
  And Perry, the peer of all these.

If Porter beheld his descendant
  With some human pride on his lip,
I trust, through the mercy of Heaven,
  His soul was forgiven that slip.

And thou, living veteran, " Old Ironsides,"
  The last of the splendid line,
Thou link 'twixt the old and new glory,
  I know what feelings were thine.

When the sun look'd over the tree-tops,
  We found ourselves—Heaven knows how—
Above the grim forts; and that instant
  A smoke broke from Farragut's bow;

And over the river came floating
  The sound of the morning gun,
And the Stars and Stripes danced up the halliards,
  And glitter'd against the sun.

Oh! then what a shout from the squadrons,
  As flag follow'd flag, till the day
Was bright with the beautiful standard,
  And wild with the victors' huzza!

But three ships were missing; the others
  Had pass'd through that current of flame;
And each scar on their shatter'd bulwarks
  Was touch'd by the finger of Fame.

Below us the forts of the rebels
  Lay in the trance of despair;
Above us, uncover'd and helpless,
  New Orleans clouded the air.

Again in long lines we went steaming
  Away towards the city's smoke;
And works were deserted before us,
  And columns of soldiers broke.

In vain the town clamor'd and struggled,
  The flag at our peak ruled the hour;
And under its shade, like a lion,
  Were resting the will and the power.

# Coming Events cast their Shadows before.

### (EXTRACT FROM MR. MURDOCH'S LECTURES.)

THE truly national lyric of "The Union," written by Francis De Haes Janvier, was first read by me in Cincinnati at the anniversary celebration of a well-known literary institution in that city. This was before the insurgents had struck the blow which left no doubt, if any had before existed in the minds of the people, of the hellish intentions of our "wayward sisters." I suggested the reading of this poem on the occasion, and referred it to the committee. Some of the members objected, not on the ground of impropriety of sentiment, but of inopportunity of occasion. The institution, it was argued, was not of a political but of a literary character, and therefore it was not expedient for it to put forth such strong sentiments at a time in which every thing should be left to the influence of conciliation and compromise. On the other hand, it was decided that the sentiment was noble and just; and as the question before the American people was not one of politics, but of right and wrong, there was no good reason to object to the assertion of *right* at any time and anywhere. The poem was read to at least two thousand people; and I can safely say that never before or since were my ears greeted with more hearty and rapturous applause than that which burst forth from an audience composed of the citizens of as loyal a city as the loyal States contain.

Mr. Janvier had the words set to music and printed on a neat enamelled card, and distributed gratuitously to the soldiers and friends of the Army of the Potomac in Washington, in the camps and the hospitals. Many and many a

7*  .

brave fellow, perchance, cheered the march to "Bull's Run," chanting the inspiring words of this song, and, it may be, died with its burden faintly but fervently breathed with his parting breath. All honor to such poets as Mr. Janvier, and to all who have, like him, devoted time and talents without stint to cheer and sustain the brave and devoted soldiers of the Republic, from the very hour in which the flag was first unfurled to the breeze in defiance to traitors, —the old flag of thirty-four stars, which, under the providence of God, shall yet wave in triumph over every State represented on its azure field, in spite of the desperate valor of the misguided men who must fall beneath the mighty power invoked by justice and legitimate authority to punish or to crush them. I will pause here to include the names of Mr. Janvier's friends and fellow-poets, Mr. Boker and Mr. Read, whose generous efforts in the same holy cause have won for them the meed of praise and honor due to patriotic acts and deeds. These gentlemen, I am proud to say, are all citizens of Philadelphia.

In lauding the patriotic efforts of the above-named gentlemen, I do not wish to be understood as speaking as one having authority in literary matters, and more especially in the poetic form, but simply as desiring to impress upon the public mind the extent and value of the services rendered to the "good cause" by the many and glorious lines they have written and placed at my disposal, so nobly calculated to keep alive the public interest in the labors I am engaged in, and to swell the current of generous and loyal sympathy in favor of the brave men who have left their homes and firesides to fight the battles of the nation.

# The Union.

## A NATIONAL SONG.

### BY FRANCIS DE HAES JANVIER.

"Liberty and Union, now and forever, one and inseparable!"—WEBSTER.

THE Union! The Union! The hope of the free!
Howsoe'er we may differ, in this we agree:—
Our glorious banner no traitor shall mar,
By effacing a stripe, or destroying a star!
Division! No, never! The Union forever!
And cursed be the hand that our country would sever!

The Union! The Union! 'Twas purchased with blood!
Side by side, to secure it, our forefathers stood:—
From the North to the South, through the length of the land,
Ran the war-cry which summon'd that patriot band!
Division! No, never! The Union forever!
And cursed be the hand that our country would sever!

The Union! The Union! At Lexington first,
Through the clouds of oppression, its radiance burst:—
But at Yorktown roll'd back the last vapory crest,
And, a bright constellation, it blazed in the West!
Division! No, never! The Union forever!
And cursed be the hand that our country would sever!

The Union! The Union! Its heavenly light
Cheers the hearts of the nations who grope in the night,—
And, athwart the wide ocean, falls, gilding the tides,
A path to the country where Freedom abides!
Division! No, never! The Union forever!
And cursed be the hand that our country would sever!

The Union! The Union! In God we repose!
We confide in the power that vanquish'd our foes!
The God of our fathers,—oh, still may He be
The strength of the Union, the hope of the free!
Division! No, never! The Union forever!
And cursed be the hand that our country would sever!

---

## The Power of Music and Verse as Incitements to Valor.

### (EXTRACT FROM MR. MURDOCH'S LECTURES.)

DURING my association with the Army of the Cumberland, in Kentucky, and while I was suffering from a severe attack of neuralgia, I was compelled to exchange the saddle for an ambulance, in which I had the good fortune to make the acquaintance of Colonel Bumford, of the regular army, who had been severely wounded at the battle of Chaplin Hills, Kentucky. I, being the least afflicted, waited on him, and endeavored to while away the time for him by reading and reciting.

I remember one evening, several officers being present in our quarters, I was asked to recite Mr. Read's war lyric of "Our Defenders." I complied; and as I turned in conclusion to the cot where the colonel lay, with his pale face and bright eyes turned towards me, he said, "Oh, Mr. Murdoch, if our brave fellows could only hear words like those on the eve of battle, how it would thrill their hearts and nerve their arms!"

He then related an incident of a charge made upon his regiment, in Mexico, in which the enemy came down upon

them with a kind of fierce chant, in which the words
"God, Santa Anna, and Liberty!" were the burden.   The
effect was exciting and grand in the extreme.

"Even our own soldiers," said he, "caught the enthusiasm, and fought with more determined valor, routing the
enemy and driving him before them."

Here, then, was a practical realization of the idea I have
endeavored to develop and enforce in my patriotic readings and recitations.   Let our poets continue to wreathe
around the national banner the ideal beauty of heroism
and self-sacrifice; let them paint, in words of fire, those
glorious sentiments which were promulgated and fought
for in 1776, contended for anew in 1812, and which
aroused the patriotic enthusiasm of the nation, sweeping
through the length and breadth of the loyal States, in
1861.   Let music add its magic force to swell the mighty
theme.   Let our soldiers learn to chant and sing such
glorious strains : then would their feet forget their weari-
ness, their hearts swell with renewed fervor, and their
arms be nerved with tenfold vigor to strike in defence
of government, laws, religious toleration, and universal
freedom.

"Our Defenders" was written by Mr. Read, in the city of
Rome, while there engaged in painting historical pictures
for some of our art-loving citizens.

It was first recited by him at a dinner given by our
minister, Mr. Cass, in Rome, on the Fourth of July following the attack on Sumter.

Mr. Read returned to this country in the following June;
since which he has served as aid and secretary to one of
our distinguished major-generals, and may yet be able to
take part in a battle and afterwards describe it, as did

Euripides, who, after leading the Grecian forces at Salamis,
wrote the tragedy of "The Persians," in which he immortal-
ized the heroic valor of the soldiers of that great republic.

## Our Defenders.

BY T. BUCHANAN READ.

OUR flag on the land and our flag on the ocean,
   An angel of peace wheresoever it goes:
Nobly sustain'd by Columbia's devotion,
    The angel of death it shall be to our foes!
      True to its native sky
      Still shall our eagle fly,
Casting his sentinel glances afar;
      Though bearing the olive-branch,
      Still in his talons staunch
Grasping the bolts of the thunders of war!

Hark to the sound! There's a foe on our border,—
   A foe striding on to the gulf of his doom;
Freemen are rising and marching in order,
   Leaving the plough and the anvil and loom.
      Rust dims the harvest-sheen
      Of scythe and of sickle keen;
The axe sleeps in peace by the tree it would mar;
      Veteran and youth are out,
      Swelling the battle-shout,
Grasping the bolts of the thunders of war!

Our brave mountain eagles swoop from their eyrie,
   Our lithe panthers leap from forest and plain;
Out of the West flash the flames of the prairie,
   Out of the East roll the waves of the main.
      Down from their Northern shores,
      Swift as Niagara pours,

They march, and their tread wakes the earth with its jar;
    Under the Stripes and Stars,
    Each, with the soul of Mars,
Grasping the bolts of the thunders of war!

Spite of the sword or assassin's stiletto,
    While throbs a heart in the breast of the brave,
The oak of the North, or the Southern palmetto,
    Shall shelter no foe except in the grave!
      While the Gulf billow breaks,
      Echoing the Northern lakes,
And ocean replies unto ocean afar,
      Yield we no inch of land
      While there's a patriot hand
Grasping the bolts of the thunders of war!

------

## Poetry and Painting as Kindred Arts.

I WILL here take occasion, in connection with the subject of Mr. Read's patriotic services, which have been many and important during the rebellion, to thank him, as well as his brother poets, for the generous aid so freely tendered me, and by which I have been enabled to keep alive the public interest in my readings and lectures.

Especially am I indebted to Mr. Read for the use of his noble and patriotic poem, "The Wagoner of the Alleghanies;" the manuscript of which he placed at my disposal in 1862, with the exclusive privilege of employing it in my "patriotic readings" for a period of not less than one year,—in the mean time foregoing the right to publish it, although offers of considerable pecuniary importance had

been made to him to induce him to give his poem to the
public at an earlier period.

It was a just and grateful tribute to the sacred Union
cemented by the blood of the fathers of 1776, to dedicate
a work commemorative of their virtues and sacrifices to
their heroic sons, who were fighting to defend the glorious
legacy bequeathed to them by their sires.

The following is a beautiful tribute to Mr. Read's professional abili-
ties. The language breathes the spirit of one fully alive to the impressions of poetry, as well as to the generous sympathy of friendship
and kindred associations; and, judging from our knowledge of Mr.
Murdoch's early professional experience, we should say that his friend's
career is as dear to him as his own. This will account for the enthusiasm and warmth of eulogy expressed in the article.—EDITOR'S NOTE.

(EXTRACT FROM MR. MURDOCH'S LECTURES.)

A poet and a painter! The qualifications which accomplish distinction in either profession are possessed by few
persons. Therefore, to attain to excellence in both is a
rare achievement. Poetry and painting, these sister arts,
are wedded to ideal passion and sublimity. They are the
handmaids to the Loves and the Graces, and they are the
recording spirits of history and fame.

The painter seizes upon all that is lovely, simple, and
grand in nature, of form and color, transferring it to his
canvas to charm the eye and delight the mind. He reproduces the rainbow hues, the mellowing tints, and sombre
shades, which compose the grandeur and simplicity of earth
and air, of sunshine and storm; and humanity owes to his
pencil the pictured lineaments of heroes and martyrs designated by the finger of Fame for the admiration and emula-
tion of man's latest posterity.

The poet, filled with that divine essence which pervades

and breathes through all the glorious works of creation, mental or physical, raises his voice in notes tuned to the music of the stars when they sang in the fulness of perfected glory, and calls on all his fellow-mortals to listen and be glad.  His song warms the heart with the genial glow of imagination and fancy, causing it to throb in unison with heroic deeds and virtuous actions.  To perfect his mastery over these attributes of the " lyre and the palette," by the exercise of his genius, has been the aim and ambition of a man glorying in the proud title of an American citizen, and honored by his loyal countrymen as an unswerving patriot and a distinguished artist.

Thomas Buchanan Read has attained to the honors of both poetry and painting in a high degree.  In boyhood a dreamer and a wanderer, he sought the far West (or what was the far West a quarter of a century since), to find amidst the excitement of artistic labor that knowledge of the world which comes to men so often through the channels of privation and suffering.

Toiling for daily bread amid the wrangle and the strife of the jostling crowd, or revelling in the bliss and beauty of nature, with no care for the present, wholly absorbed in that wealth of pleasure possessed by the youthful mind, that knows " no such word as fail," writing sonnets to ideal loveliness, and " making faces" practically, were the employments of the future man.  His pleasures in relaxation were sought, angle and line in hand, beneath the scorching sun by a meadow brook, or lounging with pen and pencil in the moist shade of some primeval forest, where tangled undergrowth and exuberant foliage served to temper the heat of the day and invite man to communion with the spirit and beauty of the Maker's works.

There is not, perhaps, a living artist in either department

8

in which Mr. Read shines so conspicuously who is so
entirely and exclusively an offspring of natural growth and
culture as is the subject of these remarks.  If they could
sit and listen, as I have done in my log cabin in the West
(till "Chanticleer has piped his challenge to the morn"), to
the fervent and eloquent pouring out of a nature "steeped
to the very lips" in poetic and pictured gifts, his readers
would know how little Mr. Read has placed on record—
although his published works are not inconsiderable—"of
that world of wealth" in the spiritual, the fanciful, and
the beautiful, by which his nature is etherealized and com-
pacted.  The wonderfully exuberant and gorgeous fancy
of Shelley, the romantic and chivalric spirit and the national
pride of Scott, and the sweetness and simplicity of Burns,
all blend and breathe in gentle sympathy in the inner life
and soul of the painter-poet,—of whom I have heard a
giant in American literature say, "His poetry is the
embodiment of nature's fanciful creation, of the exquisitely
bright and the delicately beautiful, as expressed in the loves
of the fairies and the poetry of the stars, in maiden purity
and youthful heroism.  His pictures are poems, and his
poems are pictures."

Mr. Read has not been overwhelmed with a superabun-
dance of impartial and generous notices from the public
press, in certain localities; and yet critical endorsement of
the highest and best authority has not been wanting, in
both hemispheres, to make good his title to the rank he
holds in the estimation of his admirers as one of America's
most gifted poets and distinguished painters.  The artist
who as a boy, from pure love of art, donned the staff, the
scallop-shell, and sandal shoon of the true disciple will
not be likely to weary in his pilgrimage; but, if I mistake

not the spirit of the man, he will ever be found bearing aloft the banner of his boyhood's love and ambition, "Excelsior!"

---

## Victory does not always reward Valor.

### (EXTRACT FROM MR. MURDOCH'S LECTURES.)

I SHALL never forget the pleasure with which I read Mr. Boker's poem commemorating the crossing of the Rappahannock by our brave troops under the gallant Burnside.

The soul of the true poet, burning with sympathy for heroism, romance, and chivalry, glowing with the rose-colored tints of hope and faith, poured forth all its freshness and beauty to honor the brave men who were seeking to achieve, not "the bubble reputation," but the glory and honor of their "country's cause," "in the cannon's mouth." Mr. Boker, with a generous and hopeful spirit, has caused his muse to sing the praises not only of those who have "won the battle for the free," but of those also who have valiantly fought the fight, trusting in the strength of the "God of Battles" to turn the tide of war in their favor. It was this noble impulse which prompted him to sing "Hooker's Across!" not waiting to know the result of the expedition.

And is not this the province of the poet's art,—to arouse, encourage, and sustain the warrior who draws his sword and couches his lance for justice and truth whenever the herald's trump proclaims the conflict? To win a battle is his glory; but to do or die, contending for the victory, is his honor and duty. True to his glorious mission, Mr. Boker (not in the vain spirit of boasting, but in the ardent desire to cheer and encourage) sang the praises of those who crossed the Rappahannock and struggled and bled to achieve that victory which, though it failed to alight upon our banner, refused to perch on that of the enemy. They returned, if not victorious, at least not dishonored.

Burnside and Hooker (true types of the patriot soldier) have won renown enough for their gallant soldiers to make amends for the ungenerous censure of "the people," who award no honors but where victory claims the laurel. Both of these sturdy chieftains have, since their repulse before the massed and intrenched columns of the foe at Fredericksburg and Chancellorsville, wrenched from the fickle goddess Fortune the well-earned honors of the gory field, and compelled "the many-headed and the many-minded" to bring garlands and decorate their brows, and, through them, to cheer and honor the gallant soldiers who do and die that others may live and be honored.

## The Battle of Lookout Mountain.

### BY GEO. H. BOKER.

"Give me but two brigades," said Hooker, frowning at fortified
　Lookout,
"And I'll engage to sweep yon mountain clear of that mock-
　ing rebel rout!"
At early morning came an order that set the general's face
　aglow:
"Now," said he to his staff, "draw out my soldiers. Grant
　says that I may go!"

Hither and thither dash'd each eager colonel to join his regi-
　ment,
While a low rumor of the daring purpose ran on from tent to
　tent;

For the long-roll was sounding in the valley, and the keen
   trumpet's bray,
And the wild laughter of the swarthy veterans, who cried,
   "We fight to-day!"


The solid tramp of infantry, the rumble of the great jolting
   gun,
The sharp, clear order, and the fierce steeds neighing, "Why's
   not the fight begun?"—
All these plain harbingers of sudden conflict broke on the
   startled ear;
And, last, arose a sound that made your blood leap,—the ringing battle-cheer.


The lower works were carried at one onset.   Like a vast roaring
   sea
Of steel and fire, our soldiers from the trenches swept out the
   enemy;
And we could see the gray-coats swarming up from the mountain's leafy base,
To join their comrades in the higher fastness,—for life or death
   the race!


Then our long line went winding round the mountain, in a
   huge serpent track,
And the slant sun upon it flash'd and glimmer'd, as on a
   dragon's back.
Higher and higher the column's head push'd onward, ere the
   rear moved a man;
And soon the skirmish-lines their straggling volleys and single
   shots began.


Then the bald head of Lookout flamed and bellow'd, and all
   its batteries woke,
And down the mountain pour'd the bomb-shells, puffing into
   our eyes their smoke;

And balls and grape-shot rain'd upon our column, that bore
    the angry shower
As if it were no more than that soft dropping which scarcely
    stirs the flower.

Oh, glorious courage that inspires the hero, and runs through
    all his men !
The heart that fail'd beside the Rappahannock, it was itself
    again !
The star that circumstance and jealous faction shrouded in
    envious night
Here shone with all the splendor of its nature, and with a freer
    light !

Hark ! hark ! there go the well-known crashing volleys, the
    long-continued roar,
That swells and falls, but never ceases wholly, until the fight
    is o'er.
Up towards the crystal gates of heaven ascending, the mortal
    tempest beat,
As if they sought to try their cause together before God's very
    feet!

We saw our troops had gain'd a footing almost beneath the
    topmost ledge,
And back and forth the rival lines went surging upon the
    dizzy edge.
Sometimes we saw our men fall backward slowly, and groan'd
    in our despair ;
Or cheer'd when now and then a stricken rebel plunged out
    in open air,
Down, down, a thousand empty fathoms dropping, his God
    alone knows where !

At eve, thick haze upon the mountain gather'd, with rising
    smoke stain'd black,
And not a glimpse of the contending armies shone through
    the swirling rack.

Night fell o'er all; but still they flash'd their lightnings and
    roll'd their thunders loud,
Though no man knew upon what side was going that battle in
    the cloud.

Night! what a night!—of anxious thought and wonder; but
    still no tidings came
From the bare summit of the trembling mountain, still wrapp'd
    in mist and flame.
But towards the sleepless dawn, stillness, more dreadful than
    the fierce sound of war,
Settled o'er Nature, as if she stood breathless before the morn-
    ing star.

As the sun rose, dense clouds of smoky vapor boil'd from the
    valley's deeps,
Dragging their torn and ragged edges slowly up through the
    tree-clad steeps,
And rose and rose, till Lookout, like a vision, above us grandly
    stood,
And over his black crags and storm-blanch'd headlands burst
    the warm, golden flood.

Thousands of eyes were fix'd upon the mountain, and thou-
    sands held their breath,
And the vast army, in the valley watching, seem'd touched
    with sudden death.
High o'er us soar'd great Lookout, robed in purple, a glory on
    his face,
A human meaning in his hard, calm features, beneath that
    heavenly grace.

Out on a crag walk'd something,—What? an eagle, that treads
    yon giddy height?
Surely no man! But still he clamber'd forward into the full,
    rich light;

Then up he started, with a sudden motion, and from the
    blazing crag
Flung to the morning breeze and sunny radiance the dear old
    starry flag!

Ah! then what follow'd?   Scarr'd and war-worn soldiers, like
    girls, flush'd through their tan,
And down the thousand wrinkles of the battles a thousand
    tear-drops ran;
Men seized each other in return'd embraces, and sobbed for
    very love;
A spirit which made all that moment brothers seem'd falling
    from above.

And, as we gazed, around the mountain's summit our glitter-
    ing files appear'd;
Into the rebel works we saw them marching; and we,—we
    cheer'd, we cheer'd!
And they above waved all their flags before us, and join'd our
    frantic shout,
Standing, like demigods, in light and triumph, upon their own
    Lookout!

# "The Peculiar Institution," and Stonewall Jackson's Hatred of the Old Flag.

### (EXTRACT FROM MR. MURDOCH'S LECTURES.)

I HAVE frequently been requested to recite poetry in which the heroism of rebels has been eulogized, and have always refused, on the ground that I would not acknowledge a single manly trait to exist in a traitor to his country. This rebellion is so supremely wicked and selfish, so entirely causeless upon any just grounds hitherto claimed by those who have sought the arbitration of the sword, that I would not recognize a single virtue in them, even if it existed. When has the world ever known before of a people, professing to be Christians, and claiming before the world a foremost position among the generous, the brave, the chivalrous, and the free, yet holding an inferior race in bondage, deriving all their wealth from the labor of that people, denying the slave the right of property in his own child, and rudely seizing and selling them into bondage whenever the wants of the master render it convenient and necessary,—separating man and wife, or holding all to labor and stripes without the hope of redemption, until old age secures to the worn-out carcass the right to nibble the bitter weed of the roadside and to die, while from the stores of his owner's prosperity the fruits of a long life of unrequited labor stare in his face and mock his closing eye?

When, I repeat, have we known of a people so lost to all the humanizing qualities of the heart as madly to seek at the cannon's mouth to perpetuate such unheard-of cruelties, and rudely to sever the fraternal bonds which bound them to the fellowship of those who, in compliance with the compact of their fathers, justified such injustice, at least so long as it was not allowed to gain growth and strength by sweeping over the barriers set around it to circumscribe its increase and power?

Rebellion upon just ground arises from gradually accumulated wrong and tyranny, on the part of the government, inflicted on the governed. But where the governed tyrannize over the government, the necessity for rebellion cannot exist. Conspiracy and insurrection then are the means taken to overthrow legitimate authority. Then the disaffected few inspire the many with distrust and hatred of their governors, until the public mind, restless and excited, yields to the pressure of party and faction, and becomes inflamed and bewildered with apprehensions of suffering, oppression, and tyranny. Thus the seeds of sedition and violence are sown, the weak and the ignorant misled, until the masses, gazing at that which they are told is a monster, begin to see the "horns and tail," and fly from a phantom that exists only in their own excited imagination.

The slaveholding States held within themselves the elements whence emanated that injustice and evil they falsely accused the General Government of inflicting upon them.

The institution for which they drew the sword and struck the traitorous blow was, in itself, the cause of all the trouble and discontent which excited them to rebel. Our forefathers fought the mother-country for the privilege of petition and representation; they said these were "sacred rights" of which they would not be deprived, and had Great Britain granted that right at the outset, the rebellion would have terminated before the maternal bond was severed.

The haters of tyranny and oppression in the North said, "Slavery is wrong; it ought to be restricted or abolished;" and they petitioned Congress for the privilege to debate the question. The upholders of stripes and chains in the South said, " You shall not agitate the question; you shall not petition Congress to grant the right to discuss the question. We know our Constitution provides for its own alteration and amendment; but you shall not bring before the people's representatives the subject in any form. We will hang all of you who shall come south of Mason and Dixon to argue the point, and we will bludgeon and shoot your representatives who shall dare to say that ' our mild form of holding persons to service' is oppressive or unjust."

Southern law-makers and teachers of divinity say, "It is a God-protected institution; our negroes are taught to worship God; they marry and are given in marriage, and their offspring are baptized in the Church. It is no sin," they assert, " to hold a weaker race in subjection,—to turn their sweat and blood into luxury and wealth for ourselves and our children; .and, when they dispute our right to enforce this doctrine, or are unwilling to labor, it is not oppressive or tyrannical to scourge and starve them until they become obedient. It is not wicked to part man and wife in their case. The words, ' whom God hath joined together let no man put asunder,' refer only to white people, not to negroes. 'Tis not God that joins them in marriage; their masters or mistresses only sanction the ceremonies, because, if they were really joined in accordance with God's ordinance, they could not be sold apart from each other and from their little ones." This refers more particularly to the custom on plantations. Marriage in the white church, South, means one thing, marriage in the black church, South, means another. The " man-seller" of the

South says that the negro is ordained of God for endless servitude; he was not intended for that milder form to which the Israelitish slave was consigned, and which guaranteed to the bondman, after seven years' bondage, the right to depart from his master, taking with him his wife and children, together with a portion of the worldly goods he had helped to acquire. All this was secured to him in accordance with the provisions of a merciful law, and with the blessing of the hand that bestowed it, with the assurance that there was no more servitude for him, nor for his wife, nor for their children.

Rebeldom says, "I will buy and sell the 'nigger,' chain and scourge him, as it pleases me and as my State laws permit; moreover, I will have my *righteous* right perpetuated by national legislation, so that my 'blessed institution' shall come and go hither and thither as it pleaseth it, nor shall any 'mudsill' in 'Yanl eedom' gainsay that right."

Such is the platform on which stand the insurgents of the South, and such is the attitude they maintain in the face of, and in defiance of, the whole civilized world.

"Let justice be done, though the heavens fall," saith the proverb. Then why should we not act justly, even though the slaveholder should fall? But I am talking "abolition talk," when I only meant to speak of rebels, and shall be accused of belonging to the "Wendell Phillips wing" of progress and reform.

To return to my refusal to eulogize traitors. Much has been written of the heroism and religious enthusiasm of Stonewall Jackson's character. I have no doubt that he was a conscientious man in many respects, and a Christian in a certain sense of the word; but, as he was a rebel in arms against his country, I can only afford him the acknowledgment that is expressed in the following sentiment: "When men are dead, they cease to be our enemies ;" and as Stonewall Jackson has been called to answer for his actions on earth before a higher tribunal than man's, we can afford to deal gently with his memory, and to tread lightly over his grave. The sod of his native country, saturated with the blood of her noble and loyal sons, will lie none the less heavily on the breast of one who devoted his energies and talents to strike down his countrymen who were battling in defence of human freedom, the sacred obligations of rightful allegiance, and the laws of God and man.

The beautiful and graphic picture of "Barbara Frietchie's" heroism is from the pen of John G. Whittier, the Quaker poet,—a writer whose bold and withering rebuke of injustice and error has always been as outspoken and marked as his gentle laudations of truth and honor have ever been graceful and generous. The poem is a touching tribute to the memory of one who, true to a sacred instinct of our nature, love of country,—which, properly expressed, is love of kindred and love of God,—rebuked the base and bitter spirit of the so-called Christian hero, while he was performing an act which savored of neither the spirit of a knight of chivalry nor of a soldier of God,—the only redeeming point being that he expressed his contrition for the act when a nobler nature reminded him of its baseness. As Christians we are called on to forgive our enemies; but we are not required to embalm their memories in praise or tears.

# Barbara Frietchie.

BY JOHN G. WHITTIER.

Up from the meadows rich with corn,
Clear in the cool September morn,

The cluster'd spires of Frederick stand,
Green-wall'd by the hills of Maryland.

Round about them orchards sweep,
Apple and peach tree fruited deep,

Fair as a garden of the Lord,
To the eyes of the famish'd rebel horde,

On that pleasant morn of the early Fall,
When Lee march'd over the mountain wall,

Over the mountains winding down,
Horse and foot, into Frederick town.

Forty flags with their silver stars,
Forty flags with their crimson bars,

Flapp'd in the morning wind: the sun
Of noon look'd down, and saw not one.

Up rose old Barbara Frietchie then,
Bow'd with her fourscore years and ten;

Bravest of all in Frederick town,
She took up the flag the men haul'd down.

In her attic-window the staff she set,
To show that one heart was loyal yet.

# BARBARA FRIETCHIE.

Up the street came the rebel tread,
Stonewall Jackson riding ahead.

Under his slouch'd hat left and right
He glanced: the old flag met his sight.

"Halt!"—the dust-brown ranks stood fast;
"Fire!"—out blazed the rifle-blast.

It shiver'd the window-pane and sash,
It rent the banner with seam and gash.

Quick, as it fell from the broken staff,
Dame Barbara snatch'd the silken scarf.

She lean'd far out on the window-sill,
And shook it forth with a royal will.

"Shoot, if you must, this old gray head,
But spare your country's flag," she said.

A shade of sadness, a blush of shame,
Over the face of the leader came;

The nobler nature within him stirr'd
To life at that woman's deed and word.

"Who touches a hair of yon gray head
Dies like a dog! March on!" he said.

All day long through Frederick street
Sounded the tread of marching feet;

All day long that free flag toss'd
Over the heads of the rebel host.

Ever its torn folds rose and fell
On the loyal winds that loved it well;

And, through the hill-gaps, sunset light
Shone over it with a warm good-night.

Barbara Frietchie's work is o'er,
And the rebel rides on his raids no more.

Honor to her! and let a tear
Fall, for her sake, on Stonewall's bier.

Over Barbara Frietchie's grave,
Flag of Freedom and Union, wave!

Peace and order and beauty draw
Round thy symbol of light and law;

And ever the stars above look down
On thy stars below in Frederick town.

---

## An Incident of the War.

### (EXTRACT FROM MR. MURDOCH'S LECTURES.)

"THE Sleeping Sentinel" is not alone a poem: it is an animated pageant, a series of events and incidents grouped in actual existence, moving and glowing with all the spirit of life and truth. We see, and weep for, the boy soldier Scott. We behold and mourn with his sorrow-stricken parents. How entirely do we sympathize with that soul, crushed by the weight of shame and dishonor, but not shaken by the terrors of death! We become conscious of the restless midnight step of our kind-hearted President, who, in his solitary chamber, walks pondering on the necessity of discipline and example, and the offices of gentle and lifegiving mercy. How human, too, is the shout, in which we join, to hail the coming of the glad tidings brought in the spirit of the Saviour's errand!

Without the ability or will to criticize the poet and his numbers, I simply say, I love the poem and delight in the movement of the verse. The opening words always call to my mind those peculiar and impressive lines of Dr. Holmes, addressed by the Puritan father to his son :—"Come hither, 'God be glorified,' and sit upon my knee;" not that there is any similarity in construction or sentiment, but for the savor of the old ballad-opening which hangs about them,— the old legendary bell-tone, which, like the Sabbath-tolling, seems to ring out,—

> "Come, all ye toiling people, round,
>    And unto me give ear."

Old times and old themes come forth from the mould and the dust of the past, to sun themselves in the glow of the present, when such key-notes are sounded; under their genial influence, we are moulded and impressed with the true seal of Romance and Poetry, and, like Desdemona, with a greedy ear we "devour up" the measured story.

As an illustration of this tendency of the popular heart to throb with the passion of storied verse, let me say, I have seen a thousand faces, over which were alternating the varying emotions of pride, joy, pity, and defiance, as the lookers-on sat in groups or circles on a barren hill-side (while the rebels were bombarding Chattanooga), silent and absorbed, listening to my recital of heroism, suffering, and devotion as portrayed in the ballads and lyrics of my favorite war-poets, who have sung so feelingly and fittingly of the soldier's deeds. Indeed, the attention and interest have been so profound that it might scarcely be disturbed even by the dull boom of an occasional shell bursting in the mid-air a little nearer "the audience" than the usual harmless range of Bragg's "Lookout" batteries. The tears, as they trickled down the cheeks of age and youth alike,— officers and men,—and then the shouts and cheers that would in turn burst forth as freely and unrestrainedly, all gave truthful evidence of the strong grasp fixed by the narrative and the verse on the heart and the imagination of the soldier.

Under such and other circumstances of an equally exciting character the listeners never tired of hearing "The Oath," "On Board the Cumberland, "The Sleeping Sentinel," and other poems by the same authors, many of which I have recited to citizens and soldiers, in large assemblies, amounting in the aggregate to over a hundred thousand persons.   Such poems cannot fail to excite and develop all the gentle emotions of our nature, whenever read or recited.   At the same time, they are calculated to fan the fire of patriotism in every loyal breast into a fiercer flame. They purify and elevate our moral nature, making us better and happier, casting round the social circle, the fireside-group, and the camp-gathering, a mantle of human sympathy and love.   Truly, the poet's mission is—

> "To wake the soul by tender strokes of art,
> To raise the genius, and to mend the heart."

I had the pleasure of reading this beautiful and touching poem, for the first time, to Mr. and Mrs. Lincoln, and a select party of their friends, at the White House, by invitation of Senator Foot, of Vermont, who took a great interest in the poem, not only for its high excellence, but also on account of young Scott being from his native State.

Its second reading was in the Senate-chamber of the United States, which was appropriated for the purpose,— the proceeds being for the aid of our sick and wounded soldiers.

# The Sleeping Sentinel.

BY

## FRANCIS DE HAES JANVIER,

AUTHOR OF "THE SKELETON MONK," "THE VOYAGE OF LIFE," "THE
PALACE OF THE CÆSARS," AND OTHER POEMS.

The incidents here woven into verse relate to William Scott, a young
soldier from the State of Vermont, who, while on duty as a sentinel at
night, fell asleep, and, having been condemned to die, was pardoned
by the President. They form a brief record of his humble life at home
and in the field, and of his glorious death.

> "The quality of mercy is not strain'd;
> It droppeth as the gentle rain from heaven
> Upon the place beneath: it is twice bless'd;
> It blesseth him that gives, and him that takes:
> 'Tis mightiest in the mightiest; it becomes
> The thronéd monarch better than his crown:
> His sceptre shows the force of temporal power,
> The attribute to awe and majesty,
> Wherein doth sit the dread and fear of kings;
> But mercy is above this sceptred sway,
> It is enthronéd in the hearts of kings,
> It is an attribute to God himself;
> And earthly power doth then show likest God's
> When mercy seasons justice."—SHAKSPEARE.

# The Sleeping Sentinel.

'TWAS in the sultry summer-time, as War's red records show,
When patriot armies rose to meet a fratricidal foe —
When, from the North, and East, and West, like the upheav-
    ing sea,
Swept forth Columbia's sons, to make our country truly free.

Within a prison's dismal walls, where shadows veil'd decay—
In fetters, on a heap of straw, a youthful soldier lay:
Heart-broken, hopeless, and forlorn, with short and feverish
     breath,
He waited but the appointed hour to die a culprit's death.

Yet, but a few brief weeks before, untroubled with a care,
He roam'd at will, and freely drew his native mountain air—
Where sparkling streams leap mossy rocks, from many a wood-
     land font,
And waving elms, and grassy slopes, give beauty to Vermont!

Where, dwelling in an humble cot, a tiller of the soil,
Encircled by a mother's love, he shared a father's toil—
Till, borne upon the wailing winds, his suffering country's
     cry
Fired his young heart with fervent zeal, for her to live or die.

Then left he all:—a few fond tears, by firmness half conceal'd,
A blessing, and a parting prayer, and he was in the field—
The field of strife, whose dews are blood, whose breezes War's
     hot breath,
Whose fruits are garner'd in the grave, whose husbandman is
     Death!

Without a murmur, he endured a service new and hard;
But, wearied with a toilsome march, it chanced one night, on
     guard,
He sank, exhausted, at his post, and the gray morning found
His prostrate form—a sentinel, asleep, upon the ground!

So, in the silence of the night, aweary, on the sod,
Sank the disciples, watching near the suffering Son of God;—
Yet, Jesus, with compassion moved, beheld their heavy eyes,
And, though betray'd to ruthless foes, forgiving, bade them
     rise!

But God is love,—and finite minds can faintly comprehend
How gentle Mercy, in His rule, may with stern Justice blend;
And this poor soldier, seized and bound, found none to justify,
While War's inexorable law decreed that he must die.

'Twas night.—In a secluded room, with measured tread, and
    slow,
A statesman of commanding mien, paced gravely to and fro.
Oppress'd, he ponder'd on a land by civil discord rent;
On brothers arm'd in deadly strife:—it was the President!

The woes of thirty millions fill'd his burden'd heart with grief;
Embattled hosts, on land and sea, acknowledged him their
    chief;
And yet, amid the din of war, he heard the plaintive cry
Of that poor soldier, as he lay in prison, doom'd to die!

'Twas morning.—On a tented field, and through the heated
    haze,
Flash'd back, from lines of burnish'd arms, the sun's effulgent
    blaze;
While, from a sombre prison-house, seen slowly to emerge,
A sad procession, o'er the sward, moved to a muffled dirge.

And in the midst, with faltering step, and pale and anxious
    face,
In manacles, between two guards, a soldier had his place.
A youth—led out to die;—and yet, it was not death, but
    shame,
That smote his gallant heart with dread, and shook his manly
    frame!

Still on, before the marshall'd ranks, the train pursued its
    way
Up to the designated spot, whereon a coffin lay—
His coffin! And, with reeling brain, despairing—desolate—
He took his station by its side, abandon'd to his fate!

Then came across his wavering sight strange pictures in the
    air :—
He saw his distant mountain home ; he saw his mother there ;
He saw his father bow'd with grief, through fast-declining
    years ;
He saw a nameless grave; and then, the vision closed—in
    tears !

Yet, once again.   In double file, advancing, then, he saw
Twelve comrades, sternly set apart to execute the law—
But saw no more :—his senses swam—deep darkness settled
    round—
And, shuddering, he awaited now the fatal volley's sound !

Then suddenly was heard the noise of steeds and wheels
    approach,—
And, rolling through a cloud of dust, appear'd a stately
    coach.
On, past the guards, and through the field, its rapid course was
    bent,
Till, halting, 'mid the lines was seen the nation's President !

He came to save that stricken soul, now waking from despair ;
And from a thousand voices rose a shout which rent the air !
The pardon'd soldier understood the tones of jubilee,
And, bounding from his fetters, bless'd the hand that made
    him free !

————————

'Twas Spring.—Within a verdant vale, where Warwick's
    crystal tide
Reflected, o'er its peaceful breast, fair fields on either side—
Where birds and flowers combined to cheer a sylvan solitude—
Two threatening armies, face to face, in fierce defiance stood !

Two threatening armies !   One invoked by injured Liberty—
Which bore above its patriot ranks the Symbol of the Free ;
And one, a rebel horde, beneath a flaunting flag of bars,
A fragment, torn by traitorous hands, from Freedom's Stripes
    and Stars !

A sudden shock which shook the earth, 'mid vapor dense and
    dun,
Proclaim'd, along the echoing hills, the conflict had begun;
While shot and shell, athwart the stream with fiendish fury
    sped,
To strew among the living lines the dying and the dead!

Then, louder than the roaring storm, peal'd forth the stern
    command,
"Charge! soldiers, charge!" and, at the word, with shouts, a
    fearless band,
Two hundred heroes from Vermont, rush'd onward through
    the flood,
And upward o'er the rising ground, they mark'd their way in
    blood!

The smitten foe before them fled, in terror, from his post—
While, unsustain'd, two hundred stood, to battle with a host!
Then, turning, as the rallying ranks, with murderous fire,
    replied
They bore the fallen o'er the field, and through the purple
    tide!

The fallen! And the first who fell in that unequal strife,
Was he whom Mercy sped to save when Justice claim'd his
    life—
The pardon'd soldier! And, while yet the conflict raged
    around—
While yet his life-blood ebb'd away through every gaping
    wound—

While yet his voice grew tremulous, and death bedimm'd his
    eye—
He call'd his comrades to attest he had not fear'd to die!
And, in his last expiring breath, a prayer to heaven was sent—
That God, with His unfailing grace, would bless our Presi-
    dent!

## On Board the Cumberland,

### MARCH 7, 1862.

#### BY GEORGE H. BOKER.

"*On Board the Cumberland,*" it will be observed, is in the old ballad form of verse,—that simple and unadorned style in which the deeds of Robin Hood and his merry men, and the chivalry of "Chevy Chase," won and retained the admiration of a rude age, and also that of those in which the epic, the dramatic, and the lyric forms advanced and culminated in the highest honors of the classic school of English literature. The very simplicity of the ballad form gives it the element of native energy, and as such the dramatic reader feels the full force of its surging numbers and syllabic impulses ; they enable him to gather up and hurl in a mighty mass, as it were, the soul of heroic passion, or to swell into one gushing current the tender sympathies of love and pity in extended quantities or abrupt explosions of the voice. This is the process by which the reader carries his auditor along with him, enchaining his attention, enlisting his feelings, and exciting his imagination, until the acts described, and not the manner of description, fill the eye of the mind, and the soul becomes captive to the imagery of the poet.

> " Stand to your guns, men !" Morris cried ;
>   Small need to pass the word ;
> Our men at quarters ranged themselves
>   Before the drum was heard.
>
> And then began the sailors' jests :
>   " What thing is that, I say ?"

"A 'long-shore meeting-house adrift
　Is standing down the bay!"

A frown came over Morris' face;
　The strange, dark craft he knew:
"That is the iron Merrimac,
　Mann'd by a rebel crew.

"So shot your guns and point them straight:
　Before this day goes by,
We'll try of what her metal's made."
　A cheer was our reply.

"Remember, boys, this flag of ours
　Has seldom left its place;
And where it falls, the deck it strikes
　Is cover'd with disgrace.

"I ask but this: or sink or swim,
　Or live or nobly die,
My last sight upon earth may be
　To see that ensign fly!"

Meanwhile the shapeless iron mass
　Came moving o'er the wave,
As gloomy as a passing hearse,
　As silent as the grave.

Her ports were closed; from stem to stern
　No sign of life appear'd:
We wonder'd, question'd, strain'd our eyes,
　Joked—every thing but fear'd.

She reach'd our range. Our broadside rang;
　Our heavy pivots roar'd;
And shot and shell, a fire of hell,
　Against her side we pour'd.

God's mercy! from her sloping roof
  The iron tempest glanced,
As hail bounds from a cottage-thatch,
  And round her leap'd and danced;

Or when against her dusky hull
  We struck a fair, full blow,
The mighty, solid iron globes
  Were crumbled up like snow.

On, on, with fast increasing speed,
  The silent monster came,
Though all our starboard battery
  Was one long line of flame.

She heeded not; no guns she fired;
  Straight on our bows she bore;
Through riving plank and crashing frame
  Her furious way she tore.

Alas! our beautiful, keen bow,
  That in the fiercest blast
So gently folded back the seas,
  They hardly felt we pass'd!

Alas! alas! my Cumberland,
  That ne'er knew grief before,
To be so gored, to feel so deep
  The tusk of that sea-boar!

Once more she backward drew apace;
  Once more our side she rent,
Then, in the wantonness of hate,
  Her broadside through us sent.

The dead and dying round us lay,
  But our foeman lay abeam;

Her open port-holes madden'd us,
   We fired with shout and scream.

We felt our vessel settling fast;
   We knew our time was brief:
"Ho! man the pumps!" But they who work'd,
   And fought not, wept with grief.

"Oh! keep us but an hour afloat!
   Oh! give us only time
To mete unto yon rebel crew
   The measure of their crime!"

From captain down to powder-boy,
   No hand was idle then:
Two soldiers, but by chance aboard,
   Fought on like sailor men.

And when a gun's crew lost a hand,
   Some bold marine stepp'd out,
And jerk'd his braided jacket off,
   And haul'd the gun about.

Our forward magazine was drown'd,
   And up from the sick-bay
Crawl'd out the wounded, red with blood,
   And round us gasping lay;—

Yes, cheering, calling us by name,
   Struggling with failing breath
To keep their shipmates at the post
   Where glory strove with death.

With decks afloat and powder gone,
   The last broadside we gave
From the guns' heated iron lips
   Burst out beneath the wave.

So sponges, rammers, and handspikes—
  As men-of-war's men should—
We placed within their proper racks,
  And at our quarters stood.

"Up to the spar deck! save yourselves!"
  Cried Selfridge. "Up, my men!
God grant that some of us may live
  To fight yon ship again!"

We turn'd: we did not like to go;
  Yet staying seem'd but vain,
Knee-deep in water; so we left;
  Some swore, some groan'd with pain.

We reach'd the deck. There Randall stood:
  "Another turn, men—so!"
Calmly he aim'd his pivot gun:
  "Now, Tenny, let her go!"

It did our sore hearts good to hear
  The song our pivot sang,
As rushing on from wave to wave
  The whirring bomb-shell sprang.

Brave Randall leap'd upon the gun,
  And waved his cap in sport:
"Well done! well aim'd! I saw that shell
  Go through an open port!"

It was our last, our deadliest shot;
  The deck was overflown:
The poor ship stagger'd, lurch'd to port,
  And gave a living groan.

Down, down, as headlong through the waves,
  Our gallant vessel rush'd;

A thousand gurgling watery sounds
  Around my senses gush'd.

Then I remember little more;
  One look to heaven I gave,
Where, like an angel's wing, I saw
  Our spotless ensign wave.

I tried to cheer. I cannot say
  Whether I swam or sank;
A blue mist closed around my eyes,
  And every thing was blank.

When I awoke, a soldier lad,
  All dripping from the sea,
With two great tears upon his cheeks,
  Was bending over me.

I tried to speak. He understood
  The wish I could not speak.
He turn'd me. There, thank God! the flag
  Still flutter'd at the peak!

And there, while thread shall hang to thread,
  Oh, let that ensign fly!
The noblest constellation set
  Against the northern sky,—

A sign that we who live may claim
  The peerage of the brave;
A monument that needs no scroll,
  For those beneath the wave.

## An Invocation to Loyalty.

(EXTRACT FROM MR. MURDOCH'S LECTURES.)

"THE OATH," BY THOMAS BUCHANAN READ, ESQ.

THIS poem was written by Mr. Read, a few days after the news reached Cincinnati of the brutal murder of General Robert McCook, who was shot by guerrillas, while sick and travelling, in Kentucky. It was a master-stroke of artistic effect and poetic inspiration which prompted Mr. Read to seize on the oath of the ghost in Hamlet and apply it to the sons of the men who have fought, bled, and died for our country.

Apart from the general merits of the poem, the appeal of the poet to the heroes of the past, and their answer, is intensely affecting, and reflects the highest credit upon one of the first lyrical writers of the age. I cannot refrain from referring to an exhibition of the grand and imposing effect of the recitation of this poem, under circumstances everyway calculated to test its power as an agent in arous- ·ing the sensibilities of those who are sometimes rendered, by frequent contact with violence, indifferent to the appeals of poetic imagery and inspired numbers.

While on a flying visit to my friend, General A. McDowell McCook, a few days after the battle of Chaplin Hills, in passing through Danville, Kentucky, I made a visit, in company with the general and his staff, to the house of a distinguished Kentucky statesman and loyal gentleman. While partaking of his hospitalities, and surrounded by many leading men of the neighborhood and several military gentlemen, the question of allegiance to the General

Government became the topic of discussion. Our host remarked that many of his friends, although patriotic and loyal men, were not so clear on the subject of putting down the rebellion as he could wish them to be. Upon this I remarked I did not feel disposed to argue the question in debate, but, if permitted, I would arouse their patriotic sympathies in behalf of the Government and its defenders by an invocation to duty and principle in the shape of an oath; or, in other words, I would "swear them all,"—as I possessed authority, in a poetic sense, and had the documents in my pocket. This proposition caused some astonishment, but it was agreed that I should administer the oath. I stood in the centre of a large drawing-room, or parlor, the gentlemen standing around me, and there I read the poem which is the subject of these remarks.

Intense silence pervaded the assembly during my recital, and at the close of it the entire group seemed spellbound; tears were streaming down the cheeks of many, while others, with a solemnity that marked the absorbing interest awakened by the poet, turned and grasped the hands of their neighbors. The host turned to the side-board in silence, and, as each guest raised his glass to his lips, there was a pause and a look, which seemed to render audible the words, "We swear!" while the bowed heads and measured steps of the retiring auditors as clearly expressed the sentiment of their hearts as though their tongues had uttered it.

General McCook was much affected by the recitation; and the unexpected mention of his murdered brother's name caused the gallant and impulsive soldier to shed tears, at once tender and bitter.

Who shall say that such an incident was not calculated to confirm the faith of the true patriot, and to cause the

disaffected or wavering man to think more deeply of his
duty to his country and his allegiance to that Government
under whose protection he enjoys those precious rights to
secure which his forefathers fought and bled, and for whose
perpetuation he will be held responsible by his own posterity?

## The Oath.

BY THOMAS BUCHANAN READ.

> "*Hamlet.*—Swear on my sword.
> *Ghost* (below).—Swear!"—SHAKSPEARE.

YE freemen, how long will ye stifle
  The vengeance that justice inspires?
With treason how long will ye trifle
  And shame the proud names of your sires?
Out, out with the sword and the rifle,
  In defence of your homes and your fires!
The flag of the old Revolution
  Swear firmly to serve and uphold,
That no treasonous breath of pollution
  Shall tarnish one star on its fold.
        Swear!
And hark! the deep voices replying
From graves where your fathers are lying,
    "Swear! Oh, swear!"

In this moment, who hesitates, barters
  The rights which his forefathers won;
He forfeits all claim to the charters
  Transmitted from sire to son.
Kneel, kneel at the graves of our martyrs,
  And swear on your sword and your gun;
Lay up your great oath on an altar
  As huge and as strong as Stonehenge,

And then, with sword, fire, and halter,
 Sweep down to the field of revenge,
  Swear!
And hark! the deep voices replying
From graves where your fathers are lying,
 "Swear! Oh, swear!"

By the tombs of your sires and brothers,
 The host which the traitors have slain;
By the tears of your sisters and mothers,
 In secret concealing their pain;
The grief which the heroine smothers
 Consuming the heart and the brain;
By the sigh of the penniless widow,
 By the sob of our orphans' despair,
Where they sit in their sorrowful shadow,
 Kneel, kneel, every freeman, and swear!
  Swear!
And hark! the deep voices replying
From graves where your fathers are lying,
 "Swear! Oh, swear!"

On mounds which are wet with the weeping
 Where a nation has bow'd to the sod,
Where the noblest of martyrs are sleeping,
 Let the wind bear your vengeance abroad,
And your firm oaths be held in the keeping
 Of your patriot hearts, and your God;
Over Ellsworth, for whom the first tear rose,
 While to Baker and Lyon you look,
By Winthrop, a star among heroes,
 By the blood of our murder'd McCook,
  Swear!
And hark! the deep voices replying
From graves where your fathers are lying,
 "Swear! Oh, swear!"

# Gettysburg.

(EXTRACT FROM MR. MURDOCK'S LECTURES.)

. "And he lay like a warrior taking his rest,
  With his martial cloak around him."

To stand upon what has been a great battle-field, but
what is now a vast cemetery,—to view the countless mounds
of the humble many and the decorated resting-places of
the more worldly-gifted few, and there solemnly to reflect
upon the many ills that flesh is heir to,—is to feel that war
is the monster evil that afflicts our race ; but when we look
for the cause from which arose the outpouring of that vial
of wrath, and the upheaving of that before peaceful sod,
then do we know that civil war is the lower pit of that
lowest hell depicted by the poet.

As the spectator casts his saddened eye over the rural
Golgotha, his mind, refusing to dwell too long on the stern
mementoes of human passion and frailty, arrests the thought
of the present, and he turns and gazes down the vistas of
the past.   His fancy starts at the trumpet's blast, while the
strife of battle and the roar of its fatal engines are conjured
up to his mind's eye and ear, realizing all the terrors of the
dreadful scene.   Then with an excited imagination he sits
down to think upon the seeming hollowness of glory and
the folly of war.   When he reflects, however, upon the
causes of that strife, the fruits of which are before him, he
feels that the pride of national honor inspired the brave
men who opposed that horde of rebels and of traitors, and
drove them back to starve and die amid that desolation
their own misguided counsels had produced.   Then he feels
that love of country is pride, just pride ; that a nation to
fulfil its mission must protect its honor and repel its

assailers. This is war, just war! and war is glory,—glory is the shroud as well as the banner of the hero who dies contending for his country and his God! How natural, then, is the reaction of the mind when,—leaving the sad spectacle on which his eyes have rested and over which his thoughts have wandered,—he feels his cheek glow with a just indignation at the guilt of the traitorous foe, and his heart throb with gratitude for the heroism of the loyal dead, whose glory is his country's glory and whose deeds are the embodiment of patriotism and honor. Such are the pictured scenes and solemn thoughts held up to our mental gaze in the mirror of Mr. Janvier's poem entitled "Gettysburg."

The cemetery and the battle-field are before us, and we are compelled to bow to the solemnity of the one, while we are startled and fired with the tramp and shock of the other.

I have been impressed with awe, overwhelmed with pity and grief, and excited to all the fierceness of strife, at its recital. Alternating between tears and curses, I have risen from its perusal, and felt that only a Christian spirit and a poetic inspiration combined could produce such effects upon one who has not been unaccustomed to restrain his emotions. Since my judgment first led me to admire this production of Mr. Janvier, I have found, by the intensified attention of the audiences (and they have been many and large) to whom I have recited the poem, that they responded to my own appreciation of the sentiment; while the applause that followed at the close of the recital always spoke for their estimation of the poet and the poetry.

There are few writers who possess such exquisite and delicate perceptions of the pure and the beautiful as the gentleman who is the subject of my remarks. His numbers are harmonious and flowing, and always in strict accordance with the laws of versification. If there be any objection to his poetic productions,—for I am free to confess I have not the critical ability to detect the existence of any positive one,—it may be in his over-exactness and too-sustained artistic consistency. This sometimes imparts an appearance of labored regularity to his verse, which makes us desire the use of the spur rather than the curb to the gait of his muse. But I am falling into a needless criticism of Mr. Janvier's poetry, rather than adhering to my duty of displaying its patriotic fire, heroic eulogy and Christian spirit. This I profess to accomplish by attempting through the medium of my voice a reproduction of that soul-stirring spirit which called forth the language and sentiment of a poem in which is embodied one of the most beautiful tributes that has been paid to the illustrious dead of Gettysburg,—that gallant host whose remains repose beneath the soil of their country, but whose memories are embalmed in the hearts of their countrymen. .

## Gettysburg.

### BY FRANCIS DE HAES JANVIER.

This poem is prefaced with an extract from the Farewell Address of the Father of our Country.

"The unity of Government, which constitutes you one people, is also dear to you. It is justly so; for it is a main pillar in the edifice of your real independence, the support of your tranquillity at home, your peace abroad; of your safety; of your prosperity; of that very Liberty which you so highly prize.

"But as it is easy to foresee that, from different causes and from different quarters, much pains will be taken;

many artifices employed, to weaken in your minds the conviction of this truth,—as this is the point in your political
fortress against which the batteries of internal and external
enemies will be most constantly and actively (though often
covertly and insidiously) directed, it is of infinite moment
that you should properly estimate the immense value of
your national Union to your collective and individual
happiness; that you should cherish a cordial, habitual, and
immovable attachment to it; accustoming yourselves to
think and speak of it as the palladium of your political
safety and prosperity; watching for its preservation with
jealous anxiety; discountenancing whatever may suggest
even a suspicion that it can in any event be abandoned;
and indignantly frowning upon the first dawning of every
attempt to alienate any portion of our country from the
rest, or to enfeeble the sacred ties which now link together
the various parts.

"George Washington."


Two hostile hosts are gather'd here—
  Two armies rest around;
And yet, no picket guard is near,
No pacing sentinels appear
  To watch the camping-ground!

No rattling drum, no screaming fife,
  No braying trumpet's breath,
Gives token of impending strife;
There comes no sound of martial life—
  It is the camp of Death!

The camp of Death!—The warrior's pride,
  The sword, and sash, and plume,
Are here forever laid aside—
Distinction banish'd, rank denied,
  And every tent a tomb!

Peace breathes a requiem o'er the past,
  When, down this tranquil vale,
In smoke and flame, swept war's wild blast,
While thundering guns peal'd fierce and fast,
  Through storms of iron hail!

The battle broke o'er field and grove
  Like a resistless flood,
And on through living ramparts clove,
Where Life and Death for mastery strove,
  In agony and blood!

The serried squadrons charged and fell
  Before devouring fire—
And hissing shot, and blazing shell,
Sent like some blasting bolt from hell,
  Heap'd one vast funeral pyre!

And Slaughter strew'd the purple plain
  With torture and dismay—
Till strength seem'd weak, and valor vain;
And grim and gasping, mid the slain,
  Full many a hero lay!

Then rose, with Victory's joyous tones,
  The wailings of Despair—
And mangled flesh, and shatter'd bones,
And oaths and curses, shrieks and groans,
  Commingled wildly there!

And who were those that, hand to hand,
  Thus closed in deadly strife?
Met patriots here a savage band,
Who swarm'd from some far, barbarous land,
  To strike at Freedom's life?

No!—let the infernal vaults below,
  Resound with fiendish glee—

A brother was each patriot's foe;
Fraternal hands struck every blow
  At bleeding Liberty!

Degenerate sons of sires whose names
  Undying fame shall own—
Who, in the Revolution's flames,
From fusing fetters, forged the frames
  Of Freedom's lofty throne!

Degenerate sons, who, scorn'd and bann'd,
  Eternal shame shall know—
Who, recreant to their native land,
Lured by Ambition, madly plann'd
  Their country's overthrow!

And here, upon this bloody ground,
  To Freedom consecrate—
The traitorous host advancing, found,
As mark'd henceforth, in many a mound,
  The traitor's righteous fate!

So when at first, in Heaven above,
  Foul perfidy was known—
When vile Ambition tainted love,
And impious treason rashly strove
  Against the Eternal Throne—

Before Omnipotence, dispersed,
  The rebel armies fell,
Their dazzling dreams of power reversed,
Dismay'd, defeated, crush'd, and cursed,
  And headlong hurl'd to hell!

So perish all our country's foes!—
  So ever, frustrate be
The desperate designs of those
Who, in our destiny, oppose
  God and Humanity!

Two hostile hosts are gather'd here;
   Yet, but one banner waves—
Its starry folds, now doubly dear,
Unfurl'd by Victory, appear
   Above ten thousand graves!

Two hostile hosts—but never-more
   To meet in mortal strife;
Defiance and defeat are o'er,
Nor love, nor hate, can now restore
   One prostrate form to life!

Ten thousand graves—so, far and wide,
   Before War's withering breath,
Fall friends and foes, on every side—
So rolls, through ruin, glory's tide,
   Down to the wastes of Death!

Yet here, where many a patriot fought,
   And many a martyr bled,
Shall Memory dwell—and painful thought
Will often turn, with pity fraught,
   To treason's nameless dead!

But every patriot's dust will claim
   Affection's tenderest tears—
And, blazon'd on the scroll of Fame,
Shall shine each martyr'd soldier's name
   Through Time's remotest years!

And still, upon this sacred sod,
   The children of the Free,
Who follow where our fathers trod,
Shall learn to trust our fathers' God—
   The God of Liberty!

# The School-Boy's Lesson in Poetry remembered by the Soldier on the Field of Battle.

### (EXTRACT FROM MR. MURDOCH'S LECTURES.)

I SHALL here narrate an incident of the war as an illustration of the lasting impression made on the youthful mind by the recitation of patriotic poetry, at school or elsewhere. And how true is that instinct of our nature which impels us, in moments of trial or danger, to look within ourselves or towards others for the expression of some ennobling sentiment, by which to fan the flame of heroic valor and excite the ardor of enthusiasm,—that spirit which spurs men on to dare and do in defence of principle and right!

Hence it is that, in the preparations for battle, martial music becomes a necessity. Then, too, does the language of heroism, and manly devotion in the cause we fight for, prove the steel to the flint, while the sparks that flash from the contact serve to create a flame, which, firing the veins and swelling the heart, leaves no room for the cooler faculties to operate on the nervous system. Then do men, borrowing courage from the words of heroes, burn with so fierce a flame of venturous daring that they themselves are struck with wonder when the deeds are done. The following incident I am about to relate proves how universally poetry is allied to heroic deeds, and how spontaneous is the growth of sublime courage under the excitement of danger and trial in the defence of our country's honor.

During Kirby Smith's raid in Kentucky, I was enjoying the hospitality of Colonel Jack Casement (as he is familiarly called), of the 103d Ohio. While eating our dinner

11*

of hard bread and coffee, the pickets were driven in, the order to form in line of battle was given, the trenches were manned, and, after a short speech from the Colonel, in which he exhorted his men to keep cool, load quick, and fire low, we stood awaiting the enemy, who, as we supposed, were about to make an assault upon the works from the cover of a thickly-wooded ravine on our left. My sensations were new and strange, as I had never been under fire, and, turning to the Colonel, I asked his advice as to the way in which I could be most useful to him.

He replied, "While they are advancing up the turnpike yonder, the best thing you can do will be to stand by the regimental colors and give the boys a verse or two of Marco Bozzaris,—

"'Strike!—till the last arm'd foe expires!
Strike!—for your altars and your fires!' etc.

"Do that, and, I'll pledge my life for it, there is not a drop of blood in the 103d that will not fire up and burn as long as a foe dare face them. Throw down your carbine, captain, and give us the poetry of war. That's the prelude to remind us of mother and father, of sister and brother, of our country and God! That's the music to make the boys fight, and that's the weapon you know how to strike with." I was not called upon to make the experiment; for the rebel advance we were waiting for turned out to be a party of our own forces, who, while on a reconnoissance, mistook their road. Being in a strip of wood, covered with a thick and tangled undergrowth, where the ground was broken by the winding course of a small stream, the advancing party did not realize their position until they saw the guns of Fort Mitchell frowning down upon them. Thus they narrowly escaped receiving the fiery greeting we had in readiness for the foe.

# Marco Bozzaris.

BY FITZ-GREENE HALLECK.

At midnight, in his guarded tent,
    The Turk was dreaming of the hour
When Greece, her knee in suppliance bent,
    Should tremble at his power;
In dreams, through camp and court he bore
The trophies of a conqueror;
    In dreams, his song of triumph heard;
Then wore his monarch's signet ring;
Then press'd that monarch's throne—a king:
As wild his thoughts, and gay of wing,
    As Eden's garden bird.

At midnight, in the forest shades,
    Bozzaris ranged his Suliote band,
True as the steel of their tried blades,
    Heroes in heart and hand.
There had the Persian's thousands stood,
There had the glad earth drunk their blood,
    On old Platæa's day;
And now there breathed that haunted air
The sons of sires who conquer'd there,
With arm to strike, and soul to dare,
    As quick, as far, as they.

An hour pass'd on: the Turk awoke.
    That bright dream was his last.
He woke to hear his sentries shriek,
"To arms! they come! the Greek! the Greek!"
He woke, to die 'midst flame and smoke,
And shout, and groan, and sabre-stroke,
    And death-shots falling thick and fast

As lightnings from the mountain cloud,
And heard, with voice as trumpet loud,
  Bozzaris cheer his band:
"Strike!—till the last arm'd foe expires;
Strike!—for your altars and your fires;
Strike!—for the green graves of your sires;
  God, and your native land!"

They fought like brave men, long and well;
  They piled that ground with Moslem slain;
They conquer'd;—but Bozzaris fell,
  Bleeding at every vein.
His few surviving comrades saw
His smile when rang their loud hurrah
  And the red field was won,
Then saw in death his eyelids close,
Calmly as to a night's repose,—
  Like flowers at set of sun.

Come to the bridal chamber, Death!
  Come to the mother's, when she feels,
For the first time, her first-born's breath;
  Come when the blessed seals
That close the pestilence are broke,
And crowded cities wail its stroke;
Come in consumption's ghastly form,
The earthquake shock, the ocean storm;
Come when the heart beats high and warm
  With banquet song, and dance, and wine;
And thou art terrible:—the tear,
The groan, the knell, the pall, the bier,
And all we know, or dream, or fear,
  Of agony, are thine.

But to the hero, when his sword
  Has won the battle for the free,
Thy voice sounds like a prophet's word,
And in its hollow tones are heard
  The thanks of millions yet to be.

Come when his task of fame is wrought;
Come, with her laurel-leaf, blood-bought;
  Come in her crowning hour,—and then
Thy sunken eye's unearthly light,
To him is welcome as the sight
  Of sky and stars to prison'd men;
Thy grasp is welcome as the hand
Of brother in a foreign land;
Thy summons welcome as the cry
That told the Indian isles were nigh
  To the world-seeking Genoese,
When the land-wind, from woods of palm,
And orange-groves, and fields of balm,
  Blew o'er the Haytian seas.

Bozzaris! with the storied brave
  Greece nurtured in her glory's time,
Rest thee: there is no prouder grave,
  Even in her own proud clime.
She wore no funeral weeds for thee,
  Nor bade the dark hearse wave its plume,
Like torn branch from death's leafless tree,
In sorrow's pomp and pageantry,
  The heartless luxury of the tomb;
But she remembers thee as one
Long loved, and for a season gone;
For thee her poet's lyre is wreathed,
Her marble wrought, her music breathed;
For thee she rings the birthday bells;
Of thee her babes' first lisping tells;
For thine her evening prayer is said,
At palace couch and cottage bed;
Her soldier, closing with the foe,
Gives for thy sake a deadlier blow;
His plighted maiden, when she fears
For him, the joy of her young years,
Thinks of thy fate, and checks her tears;

And she, the mother of thy boys,
Though in her eye and faded cheek
Is read the grief she will not speak,
The memory of her buried joys,—
And even she who gave thee birth,
Will, by their pilgrim-circled hearth,
Talk of thy doom without a sigh ;
For thou art Freedom's now, and Fame's.
One of the few, the immortal names
That were not born to die.

---

## Heroes Die, but Heroism is Eternal.

### (EXTRACT FROM MR. MURDOCH'S LECTURES.)

ON the 21st of February, 1862, a battle was fought in
Texas between the Federal forces and the Rebels.  Captain
McRea, of the Federal artillery, was in command of a battery supported by a force of New Mexican levies.  The
Texan Rangers made a dash for the guns : the infantry
gave way and ingloriously fled at the first charge, thus
leaving the battery unsupported.  Nothing daunted, the
gallant McRea fought on until, finding himself surrounded,
and seeing no chance of redeeming the fortunes of the
day, in defiance of the summons to surrender, he drew his
revolvers, and, leaping on one of his guns, maintained the
fight, falling in the midst of foes, covered with wounds,—
thus gallantly sealing with his blood his fidelity to his
country's cause.  Who would withhold from such valor the
meed of praise, or feel his pulse beat sluggishly when the
poet sings in glowing strains the gloirous deeds of those
who die in defence of country and Government, covered
with the benediction of a sorrowing people?

The circumstances attending the glorious death of the hero of our fight, and that of the hero of Mr Boker's poem, are the property of different ages and of different nations; yet the soul which shines through them belongs to all time and all nations : it is the generous outpouring of that spirit which burns in the bosom of every man loyal to honor, to woman, and to country, and which sustains the possessor in every trial of danger and of suffering, and in the solemn hour of death. True honor and chivalry are the same now as they were in the days of romance, and are always found beneath the banners on which are emblazoned Justice, Truth, and Virtue ; and there, till Fame's trump shall sound no more, will be found such glorious and self-sacrificing champions as Olea and McRea.

## Count Candespina's Standard.

### BY GEORGE H. BOKER.

"THE King of Aragon now entered Castile by way of Soria and Osma with a powerful army; and, having been met by the queen's forces, both parties encamped near Sepulveda, and prepared to give battle.

"This engagement, called, from the field where it took place, *de la Espina*, is one of the most famous of that age. The dastardly Count of Lara fled at the first shock, and joined the queen at Burgos, where she was anxiously awaiting the issue ; but the brave Count of Candespina (Gomez Gonzalez) stood his ground to the last, and died on the field of battle. His standard-bearer, a gentleman of the house of Olea, after having his horse killed under him, and both hands cut off by sabre-strokes, fell beside his master, still clasping the standard in his arms, and repeating his war-cry of 'Olea!'"—MRS. GEORGE: *Annals of the Queen of Spain.*

> SCARCE were the splinter'd lances dropp'd,
> Scarce were the swords drawn out,
> Ere recreant Lara, sick with fear,
> Had wheel'd his steed about ;

His courser rear'd, and plunged, and neigh'd,
  Loathing the fight to yield;
But the coward spurr'd him to the bone,
  And drove him from the field.

Gonzalez in his stirrups rose:
  " Turn, turn, thou traitor knight!
Thou bold tongue in a lady's bower,
  Thou dastard in a fight!"

But vainly valiant Gomez cried
  Across the waning fray:
Pale Lara and his craven band
  To Burgos scour'd away.

"Now, by the God above me, sirs,
  Better we all were dead,
Than a single knight among ye all
 * Should ride where Lara led!

" Yet, ye who fear to follow me,
  As yon traitor turn and fly;
For I lead ye not to win a field:
  I lead ye forth to die.

"Olea, plant my standard here,
  Here, on this little mound;
Here raise the war-cry of thy house,
  Make this our rallying ground.

"Forget not, as thou hop'st for grace,
  The last care I shall have,
Will be to hear thy battle-cry,
  And see that standard wave."

Down on the ranks of Aragon
  The bold Gonzalez drove,
And Olea raised his battle-cry,
  And waved the flag above.

Slowly Gonzalez' little band
　Gave ground before the foe ;
But not an inch of the field was won
　Without a deadly blow ;

And not an inch of the field was won
　That did not draw a tear
From the widow'd wives of Aragon,
　That fatal news to hear.

Backward and backward Gomez fought,
　And high o'er the clashing steel,
Plainer and plainer, rose the cry,
　"Olea for Castile !"

Backward fought Gomez, step by step,
　Till the cry was close at hand,
Till his dauntless standard shadow'd him ;
　And there he made his stand.

Mace, sword, and axe rang on his mail,
　Yet he moved not where he stood,
Though each gaping joint of armor ran
　A stream of purple blood.

As, pierced with countless wounds, he fell,
　The standard caught his eye,  ˙
And he smiled, like an infant hush'd asleep,
　To hear the battle-cry.

Now one by one the wearied knights
　Have fallen, or basely flown ;
And on the mound where his post was fix'd
　Olea stood alone.

" Yield up thy banner, gallant knight !
　Thy lord lies on the plain ;
Thy duty has been nobly done ;
　I would not see thee slain."

12

"Spare pity, King of Aragon;
  I would not hear thee lie: .
My lord is looking down from heaven,
  To see his standard fly."

"Yield, madman, yield!—Thy horse is down,
  Thou hast nor lance nor shield;
Fly!—I will grant thee time."—"This flag
  Can neither fly nor yield!"

They girt the standard round about,
  A wall of flashing steel;
But still they heard the battle-cry,  ˙
  "Olea for Castile!"

And there, against all Aragon,
  Full-arm'd with lance and brand,
Olea fought until the sword
  Snapp'd in his sturdy hand.

Among the foe, with that high scorn
  Which laughs at earthly fears,
He hurl'd the broken hilt, and drew
  His dagger on the spears.

They hew'd the hauberk from his breast,
  The helmet from his head,
They hew'd the hands from off his limbs,
  From every vein he bled.

Clasping the standard to his heart,
  He raised one dying peal,
That rang as if a trumpet blew,—
  "Olea for Castile!"

### Don't Give Up the Ship.

(EXTRACT FROM MR. MURDOCH'S LECTURES.)

"THE Building of the Ship" is one of the most brilliant productions of one of America's most gifted poets. The apostrophe to the Union cannot be excelled: it is the perfection of numbers, and the acme of Saxon simplicity, terseness, and force, combining fervent dignity with the pure spirit of the patriot.

It is, indeed, an eloquent outpouring of a truly loyal heart. When we reflect upon the fact that it was written several years since, it seems like a trumpet-tone borne to us on the wings of the wind, from the depths of that storm-cloud which began to gather on the national horizon long before the Ship of State drifted among the breakers which now threaten her on every side.

The prescience of the poet failed to warn us of the approaching danger: let it at least inspire us with manly courage and devoted patriotism, to breast the storm and struggle through its howling terrors, until blue skies and gentle ripples bless once more the mighty ocean of our nation's destiny.

This is the purpose I have in view in ringing in your ears, with all the fervor and the skill I may possess, the noble and sustaining language of Longfellow and other kindred spirits, and more especially of those American poets who have, during the rebellion, strode in advance of our armies, striking the lyre, and singing the praises of heroism, fortitude, and self-sacrifice,—virtues that have been nobly and freely offered in the service of our beloved country by her brave and suffering defenders. We must not lose sight of, or grow weary with, the often-uttered but still fresh and grandly inspiring sentiment of our war-poets. The music of the lyre, the trumpet, and the drum must still vibrate in the nation's ear to keep alive the sentiment of national glory, to nerve the arm and fire the heart in this great struggle of freedom with its original and brutal foe, selfish power, and its vile supporters, the scourge and the chain.

It does not need my voice to inform you of the perilous sea on which our national bark is afloat. The roar of battle-fields, the groans of the wounded borne to us on every wind, mingling with the wailings of widows and orphans, fill the air, clouding the brow and saddening the heart of every loyal citizen.

To weather this fearful sea of strife and carnage, we must pull together, heart and hand. "A long pull, and a strong pull, with a will!" is the cry now. As loyal and union-loving Americans, we are all passengers in the glorious Ship of State, "The Union." We are in the midst of a fearful storm, breakers ahead, false lights on the coast, and a lee shore: nothing but courage and unity of action can save us. There is mutiny aboard; the whispering of the malcontents is hissing in our ears on every side; while bold, bad men are counselling desertion of the colors, and, instead of trusting to the will and skill of the officers and crew to bring the vessel off, seek rather to run her ashore, trusting to the chances of the wrecker's spoils and plundering.

"Don't give up the ship!" cried Lawrence, as his men carried him, bleeding, below. "The Stars and Stripes must not come down," cried Blake, as, in obedience to his orders, the brave tars quickened their fire when the little Hatteras began to sink alongside the worse than pirate Alabama.

So, my friends, let the war-cry of the Union-man be, "Defiance to all traitors, North or South! our colors are nailed to the mast; we will sink or swim with our ship, and never desert captain, pilot, or crew!"

To those who are base enough in their own natures to lead, or weak enough to be guided by bad men, in the attempt to cripple the Government and strengthen its foes, by abuse of the one and encouragement of the other, I would, in the spirit of love and good will to my fellow-men, say, "When a ship is laboring with the tempestuous ocean, when all the elements and all their angers are turned into one vowed destruction,"—is such a fitting time to arraign the officers before a tribunal of the passengers, to answer for the safety of the life and the property which has been intrusted to their charge? Would it not be the more humane, if not the more consistent, course, to await the issue calmly and hopefully, trusting to the discretion of a divine power and the honest and brave endeavors of the few selected from the many and invested with authority to direct and control?

Then let us, my friends, instead of charging our rulers with weakness and folly and a base and wicked intent to forsake the course indicated by the compass and line of constitutional direction, endeavor to cheer our leaders, amid the gloom and terrors of the storm, with words of trust and confidence.

Let us call on them to join with us in seeking aid and counsel from Him who holds the winds in the hollow of His hand; to humbly seek from Him that strength and will and knowledge by which the most intricate chart is read aright, and the hand made firm on the helm in the midst of the darkest terrors.

Yes, my countrymen, "come what come may," let us
12*

stand by the ship; and, if need be (rather than surrender), let us go down with her, even as Morris and his brave men did on board the Cumberland. They sank at their posts, flashing forth their defiant death-notes till the last, leaving nothing but the "flag at the peak" to silently tell, in sunshine and in storm, of the deadly struggle between traitors and the brave men who died defending the priceless boon bequeathed to United America by the patriotic sires of 1776.

---

## The Launching of the Ship.

AN EXTRACT FROM THE POEM OF "THE BUILDING OF THE SHIP.")

BY LONGFELLOW.

To-DAY the vessel shall be launch'd.
With fleecy clouds the sky is blanch'd,
And o'er the bay,
Slowly, in all his splendors dight,
The great sun rises to behold the sight.
The ocean old,
Centuries old,
Strong as youth, and as uncontroll'd,
Paces restless to and fro
Up and down the sands of gold.
His beating heart is not at rest;
And far and wide,
With ceaseless flow,
His beard of snow
Heaves with the heaving of his breast.
He waits impatient for his bride.

There she stands,
With her foot upon the sands,
Deck'd with flags and streamers gay,
In honor of her marriage-day,
Her snow-white signals fluttering, blending,
Round her like a veil descending,
Ready to be
The bride of the gray old sea.

On the deck another bride
Is standing by her lover's side.
Shadows from the flags and shrouds,
Like the shadows cast by clouds,
Broken by many a sunny fleck,
Fall around them on the deck.

The prayer is said,
The service read,
The joyous bridegroom bows his head,
And in tears the good old master
Shakes the brown hand of his son,
Kisses his daughter's glowing cheek
In silence, for he cannot speak;
And ever faster
Down his own the tears begin to run.
The worthy pastor—
The shepherd of that wandering flock,
That has the ocean for its wold,
That has the vessel for its fold,
Leaping ever from rock to rock,—
Spake, with accents mild and clear,
Words of warning, words of cheer,
But tedious to the bridegroom's ear.
He knew the chart
Of the sailor's heart,
All its pleasures and its griefs,
All its shallows and rocky reefs,

All those secret currents that flow
With such resistless undertow,
And lift and drift, with terrible force,
The will from its moorings and its course:
Therefore he spoke, and thus said he:—

"Like unto ships far off at sea,
Outward or homeward bound are we.
Before, behind, and all around
Floats and swings the horizon's bound.
Seems at its distant rim to rise
And climb the crystal wall of the skies,
And then again to turn and sink,
As if we could slide from its outer brink.
Ah! it is not the sea,
It is not the sea that sinks and shelves,
But ourselves,
That rock and rise
With endless and uneasy motion,
Now touching the very skies,
Now sinking into the depths of ocean.
Ah! if our souls but poise and swing,
Like the compass in its brazen ring,
Ever level and ever true
To the toil and task we have to do,
We shall sail securely, and safely reach
The Fortunate Isles, on whose shining beach
The sights we see, and the sounds we hear,
Will be those of joy, and not of fear."

Then the master,
With a gesture of command,
Waved his hand;
And, at the word,
Loud and sudden there was heard,
All around them and below,
The sound of hammers, blow on blow,

Knocking away the shores and spurs.
And see! she stirs!
She starts; she moves; she seems to feel
The thrill of life along her keel,
And, spurning with her foot the ground,
With one exulting, joyous bound
She leaps into the ocean's arms!
And, lo! from the assembled crowd
There rose a shout, prolong'd and loud,
That to the ocean seemed to say,
"Take her, O bridegroom old and gray,—
Take her to thy protecting arms,
With all her youth and all her charms!"

How beautiful she is! How fair
She lies within those arms that press
Her form with many a soft caress
Of tenderness and watchful care!
Sail forth into the sea, O ship!
Through wind and wave right onward steer!
The moisten'd eye, the trembling lip,
Are not the signs of doubt or fear.

Sail forth into the sea of life,
O gentle, loving, trusting wife,
And safe from all adversity
Upon the bosom of that sea
Thy comings and thy goings be!
For gentleness, and love, and trust
Prevail o'er angry wave and gust;
And in the wreck of noble lives,
Something immortal still survives.

Thou too sail on, O Ship of State!
Sail on, O Union, strong and great!
Humanity, with all its fears,
With all the hopes of future years,

Is hanging breathless on thy fate!
We know what master laid thy keel,
What workman wrought thy ribs of steel,
Who made each mast, and sail, and rope,
What anvils rang, what hammers beat,
In what a forge and what a heat
Were shaped the anchors of thy hope.
Fear not each sudden sound and shock:
'Tis of the wave, and not the rock;
'Tis but the flapping of the sail,
And not a rent made by the gale!
In spite of rock and tempest's roar,
In spite of false lights on the shore,
Sail on, nor fear to breast the sea!
Our hearts, our hopes, are all with thee:
Our hearts, our hopes, our prayers, our tears,
Our faith triumphant o'er our fears,
Are all with thee! are all with thee!

---

# The Dying Soldier.

### BY RICHARD COE.

"CHAPLAIN, I am dying, dying:
　　Cut a lock from off my hair,
For my darling mother, chaplain,
　　After I am dead, to wear:
Mind you, 'tis for mother, chaplain,
　　She whose early teachings now
Soothe and comfort the poor soldier
　　With the death-dew on his brow!

"Kneel down, now, beside me, chaplain,
　　And return my thanks to Him

Who so good a mother gave me:
    Oh, my eyes are growing dim!
Tell her, chaplain, should you see her,
    All at last with me was well;
Through the valley of the shadow
    I have gone, with Christ to dwell!

"Do not weep, I pray you, chaplain:
    Yes, ah! weep for mother dear;
I'm the only living son, sir,
    Of a widow'd mourner here:
Mother! I am going, going
    To the land where angels dwell;
I commend you unto Jesus:
    Mother darling—fare you well!"

Downward from their thrones of beauty
    Look'd the stars upon his face;
Upward on the wings of duty
    Sped the angel of God's grace,
Bearing through the heavenly portal,
    To his blessed home above,
The dead soldier's soul immortal,
    To partake of Christ's sweet love.

Far away, in humble cottage,
    Sits his mother, sad and lone;
And her eyes are red with weeping,
    Thinking of her absent son:
Suddenly Death's pallid presence
    Casts a shadow o'er her brow:
Smiling a sweet smile of welcome,
    She is with her loved ones now!

## The Rising, 1776.

(EXTRACT FROM "THE WAGONER OF THE ALLEGHANIES.")

BY T. BUCHANAN READ.

OUT of the North the wild news came,
Far flashing on its wings of flame,
Swift as the boreal light which flies
At midnight through the startled skies.

And there was tumult in the air,
   The fife's shrill note, the drum's loud beat,
And through the wide land everywhere
   The answering tread of hurrying feet;
While the first oath of Freedom's gun
Came on the blast from Lexington;
And Concord roused, no longer tame,
Forgot her old baptismal name,
Made bare her patriot arm of power,
And swell'd the discord of the hour.

Within its shade of elm and oak
   The church of Berkley Manor stood;
There Sunday found the rural folk,
   And some esteem'd of gentle blood.
   In vain their feet with loitering tread
Pass'd mid the graves where rank is naught;
All could not read the lesson taught
   In that republic of the dead.

How sweet the hour of Sabbath talk,
   The vale with peace and sunshine full,
Where all the happy people walk,
   Deck'd in their homespun flax and wool!
   Where youth's gay hats with blossoms bloom;

And every maid, with simple art,
Wears on her breast, like her own heart,
  A bud whose depths are all perfume;
While every garment's gentle stir
Is breathing rose and lavender.


There, veil'd in all the sweets that are
  Blown from the violet's purple bosom,
The scent of lilacs from afar,
  Touch'd with the sweet shrub's spicy blossom,
Walk'd Esther; and the rustic ranks
Stood on each side, like flowery banks,
To let her pass,—a blooming aisle,
Made brighter by her summer smile;
On her father's arm she seem'd to be
The last green bough of that haughty tree.


The pastor came; his snowy locks
  Hallow'd his brow of thought and care;
And calmly, as shepherds lead their flocks,
  He led into the house of prayer.
  Forgive the student Edgar there
If his enchanted eyes would roam,
  And if his thoughts soar'd not beyond,
  And if his heart glow'd warmly fond
Beneath his hope's terrestrial dome.
To him the maiden seem'd to stand,
  Veil'd in the glory of the morn,
  At the bar of the heavenly bourn,
A guide to the golden holy land.
  When came the service low response,
Hers seem'd an angel's answering tongue;
When with the singing choir she sung,
O'er all the rest her sweet notes rung,
As if a silver bell were swung
  Mid bells of iron and of bronze.

13

At times, perchance,—oh, happy chance!—
  Their lifting eyes together met,
  Like violet to violet,
Casting a dewy greeting glance.
For once be Love, young Love, forgiven,
  That here, in a bewilder'd trance,
  He brought the blossoms of romance,
And waved them at the gates of heaven.

The pastor rose; the prayer was strong;
The psalm was warrior David's song;
The text, a few short words of might,—
"The Lord of hosts shall arm the right!"
He spoke of wrongs too long endured,
Of sacred rights to be secured;
Then from his patriot tongue of flame
The startling words for Freedom came.
The stirring sentences he spake
Compell'd the heart to glow or quake,
And, rising on his theme's broad wing,
  And grasping in his nervous hand
  The imaginary battle-brand,
In face of death he dared to fling
Defiance to a tyrant king.

Even as he spoke, his frame, renewed
In eloquence of attitude,
Rose, as it seem'd, a shoulder higher;
Then swept his kindling glance of fire
From startled pew to breathless choir;
When suddenly his mantle wide
His hands impatient flung aside,
And, lo! he met their wondering eyes
Complete in all a warrior's guise.

A moment there was awful pause,—
When Berkley cried, "Cease, traitor! cease!

God's temple is the house of peace!"
  The other shouted, "Nay, not so,
When God is with our righteous cause;
His holiest places then are ours,
His temples are our forts and towers
  That frown upon the tyrant foe;
In this, the dawn of Freedom's day,
There is a time to fight and pray!"

And now before the open door—
  The warrior priest had order'd so—
The enlisting trumpet's sudden roar
Rang through the chapel, o'er and o'er,
  Its long reverberating blow,
So loud and clear, it seem'd the ear
Of dusty death must wake and hear.
And there the startling drum and fife
Fired the living with fiercer life;
While overhead, with wild increase,
Forgetting its ancient toll of peace,
  The great bell swung as never before
It seem'd as it would never cease;
And every word its ardor flung
From off its jubilant iron tongue
  Was, "War! war! war!"

"Who dares?"—this was the patriot's cry,
  As striding from the desk he came,—
  "Come out with me, in Freedom's name,
For her to live, for her to die?"
A hundred hands flung up reply,
A hundred voices answer'd, "I!"

## Before Vicksburg.

(MAY 19, 1863.)

THE President has recently appointed to the Naval
School at Newport a little drummer-boy of the 55th Illinois
Volunteers, whose case was brought before him by Major-
General W. T. Sherman in the following letter.   Truly,
the letter does as much honor to the distinguished major-
general, who could pause in the midst of the duties of a
great campaign to pay such tribute to a drummer-boy, as
it does to the little hero whom it celebrates :—

"HEAD-QUARTERS 15TH ARMY CORPS,<br>
"CAMP ON BIG BLACK RIVER, August 8, 1863.

"HON. E. M. STANTON, *Secretary of War :—*

"SIR:—I take the liberty of asking through you that something be done for a lad named Orion P. Howe, of Waukegan,
Illinois, who belongs to the 55th Illinois, but at present at
home wounded.   I think he is too young for West Point, but
would be the very thing for a midshipman.

"When the assault at Vicksburg was at its height, on the
19th of May, and I was in front near the road, which formed
my line of attack, this young lad came up to me, wounded and
bleeding, with a good, healthy boy's cry, 'General Sherman,
send some cartridges to Colonel Malmborg : the men are nearly
all out.'   'What is the matter, my boy?'   'They shot me in
the leg, sir ; but I can go to the hospital.   Send the cartridges
right away.'   Even where we stood the shot fell thick, and I
told him to go to the rear at once, I would attend to the cartridges ; and off he limped.   Just before he disappeared on the
hill, he turned, and called, as loud as he could, 'Calibre 54.'   I
have not seen the lad since, and his colonel (Malmborg), on

inquiry, gives me the address as above, and says he is a bright, intelligent boy, with a fair preliminary education.

"What arrested my attention then was—and what renewed my memory of the fact now is—that one so young, carrying a musket-ball through his leg, should have found his way to me on that fatal spot, and delivered his message, not forgetting the very important part, even, of the calibre of his musket,—54,— which, you know, is an unusual one.

"I'll warrant that the boy has in him the elements of a man, and I commend him to the Government as one worthy the fostering care of some one of its national institutions.

"I am, with respect, your obedient servant,

"W. T. SHERMAN,
*Major-General Commanding.*"


WHILE Sherman stood beneath the hottest fire
  That from the lines of Vicksburg gleam'd,
And bomb-shells tumbled in their smoky gyre,
  And grape-shot hiss'd, and case-shot scream'd,
      Back from the front there came,
      Weeping and sorely lame,
  The merest child, the youngest face,
  Man ever saw in such a fearful place.

Stifling his tears, he limp'd his chief to meet;
  But, when he paused and tottering stood,
Around the circle of his little feet
  There spread a pool of bright young blood.
      Shock'd at his doleful case,
      Sherman cried, "Halt! front face!
  Who are you? speak, my gallant boy!"
  "A drummer, sir,—Fifty-fifth Illinois."

"Are you not hit?" "That's nothing. Only send
  Some cartridges. Our men are out,
And the foe press us." "But, my little friend——"
  "Don't mind me! Did you hear that shout?

What if our men be driven?
   Oh, for the love of heaven,
Send to my colonel, general dear——"
"But you?"——"Oh, I shall easily find the rear."

"I'll see to that," cried Sherman; and a drop,
   Angels might envy, dimm'd his eye,
As the boy, toiling towards the hill's hard top,
   Turn'd round, and, with his shrill child's cry,
     Shouted, "Oh, don't forget!
     We'll win the battle yet!
But let our soldiers have some more—
More cartridges, sir,—calibre fifty-four!"

                  GEORGE H. BOKER.

April 2, 1864.

---

## Our Heroes.

BY FRANCIS DE HAES JANVIER.

CHEERS! Cheers for our heroes;
   Not those who wear stars;
Nor those who wear eagles,
   And leaflets, and bars;
We know they are gallant,
   And honor them, too,
For bravely maintaining
   The Red, White, and Blue!

But, cheers for our soldiers,
   Rough, wrinkled, and brown;
The men who MAKE heroes,
   And ask no renown:—
Unselfish, untiring,
   Intrepid, and true;
The bulwark surrounding
   The Red, White, and Blue!

Our patriot soldiers !
　When Treason arose,
And Freedom's own children
　Assail'd her as foes ;
When Anarchy threaten'd,
　And Order withdrew,
They rallied to rescue
　The Red, White, and Blue !

Upholding our banner,
　On many a field,
The doom of the traitor
　They valiantly seal'd ;
And, worn with the conflict,
　Found vigor anew,
Where Victory greeted
　The Red, White, and Blue !

Yet, loved ones have fallen—
　And still, where they sleep
A sorrowing Nation
　Shall silently weep ;
And Spring's fairest flowers,
　In gratitude, strew,
O'er those who have cherish'd
　The Red, White, and Blue !

But, glory immortal
　Is waiting them now ;
And chaplets unfading,
　Shall bind every brow,
When, call'd by the trumpet,
　At Time's great review,
They stand, who defended
　The Red, White, and Blue !

## Wounded.

BY REV. WILLIAM E. MILLER.

LET me lie down
Just here in the shade of this cannon-torn tree,
Here, low on the trampled grass, where I may see
The surge of the combat, and where I may hear
The glad cry of victory, cheer upon cheer:
      Let me lie down.

      Oh, it was grand!
Like the tempest we charged, in the triumph to share;
The tempest,—its fury and thunder were there:
On, on, o'er intrenchments, o'er living and dead,
With the foe under foot, and our flag overhead:
      Oh, it was grand!

      Weary and faint,
Prone on the soldier's couch, ah, how can I rest,
With this shot-shatter'd head and sabre-pierced breast?
Comrades, at roll-call when I shall be sought,
Say I fought till I fell, and fell where I fought,
      Wounded and faint.

      Oh, that last charge!
Right through the dread hell-fire of shrapnel and shell,
Through without faltering,—clear through with a yell!
Right in their midst, in the turmoil and gloom,
Like heroes we dash'd, at the mandate of doom!
      Oh, that last charge!

      It was duty!
Some things are worthless, and some others so good
That nations who buy them pay only in blood.

For Freedom and Union each man owes his part;
And here I pay my share, all warm from my heart:
        It is duty.

        Dying at last!
My mother, dear mother! with meek tearful eye,
Farewell! and God bless you, for ever and aye!
Oh that I now lay on your pillowing breast,
To breathe my last sigh on the bosom first prest!
        Dying at last!

        I am no saint;
But, boys, say a prayer.   There's one that begins,
"Our Father," and then says, "Forgive us our sins:"
Don't forget that part, say that strongly, and then
I'll try to repeat it, and you'll say, " Amen!"
        Ah! I'm no saint!

        Hark! there's a shout!
Raise me up, comrades!   We have conquer'd, I know!—
Up, up on my feet, with my face to the foe!
Ah! there flies the flag, with its star-spangles bright,
The promise of glory, the symbol of right!
        Well may they shout!

        I'm muster'd out.
O God of our fathers, our freedom prolong,
And tread down rebellion, oppression, and wrong!
O land of earth's hope, on thy blood-redden'd sod
I die for the nation, the Union, and God!
        I'm muster'd out.

(From the "Cincinnati Daily Commercial," Tuesday Morning, January 19, 1864.)

## An Old Friend in a New Dress.

(Sung to the tune of "Hurrah for the Bonnets of Blue.")

"On the first page will be found a song that sings itself, adapted from Burns's 'Here's a Health to Them that's Awa',' by James E. Murdoch, Esq. The original song was not published during the life of Burns. It was first given to the public in 1818, in the 'Edinburgh Magazine,' and was incorporated the following year into a small edition of his writings published at Melrose by John Smith, bookseller. A political song, it breathes the spirit of good-fellowship, and an admiration for honest purpose, patriotic devotion to country and freedom, and whatever is honorable or noble in man or woman. It has lost none of its vigor of expression, the perfection of its rhythm, or its patriotic spirit, by Mr. Murdoch's felicitous adaptation."

### "HERE'S A HEALTH TO THEM THAT'S AWA'."

Lines by Robert Burns, altered and adapted to suit the present times, by James E. Murdoch, with an apology for the liberty taken with the original song,—a liberty which nothing but a truly loyal object could justify.

> Here's a health to them that's awa',
>     And here's to them that's awa';
> And wha would na' wish guid luck to our cause,
>     May never guid luck be their fa'!
> It's guid to be merry and wise,
>     It's guid to be honest and true;
> It's guid to support Columbia's cause,
>     And bide by the Red, White, and Blue.
> *Chorus.*—Hurrah for the Red, White, and Blue!
>     Hurrah for the Red, White and Blue!
> It's guid to support our country's cause,
>     And bide by the Red, White, and Blue.

Here's a health to them that's awa',
And here's to them that's awa';
Here's a health to "auld Abe," the chief o' the clan,
And may his band never be sma'!
May Liberty meet wi' success;
May prudence protect her fra' evil;
May traitors and tyranny tine* i' the mist,
And wander their way to the de'il.
*Chorus.*—Hurrah for the Red, White, and Blue! &c.


Here's a health to them that's awa',
And here's to them that's awa';
Here's a bumper to Chase,—he, the Western laddie,
That made "Greenbacks" as guid as the law.
Here's freedom to him that would read,
Here's freedom to him that would write:
There's nane ever fear'd that the truth should be heard,
But they wham the truth would indict.
*Chorus.*—Hurrah for the Red, White, and Blue! &c.


Here's a health to them that's awa',
And here's to them that's awa';
Here's Meade, and here's Grant; and wha would them daunt,
We'll build in a hole i' the wa'.
Here's woman that's true at the heart,
Here's man that is sound at the core:
May he that wad turn his button and coat
Be turn'd to the back of the door.
*Chorus.*—Hurrah for the Red, White, and Blue! &c.


Here's a health to them that's awa',
And here's to them that's awa';
Here's Abram Lincoln, a chief that's na' winkin',
But bred wi' an axe in his paw;

---

* Be lost.

Here's friends to the Stripes and the Stars,
  Here's friends that stand by them at need;
And wha would betray his country's cause
  May hang by the neck till he's deed.
*Chorus.*—Hurrah for the Red, White, and Blue! &c.

Here's a health to them that's awa',
  And here's to them that's awa';
Here's a health to *our uncle*,—to guid *Uncle Sam,*
  His soldiers and sailors so braw!
May cruel *war* soon be over,
  And peace to our land come again;
May law and unity triumph,
  And banish all sorrow and pain!
*Chorus.*—Hurrah for the Red, White, and Blue! &c.

---

## Lines on the New American Frigate Alliance.

BY PHILLIP FRENEAU, A POET OF THE REVOLUTION, 1776.

As Neptune traced the azure main,
That own'd so late proud Britain's reign,
A floating pile approach'd his car,—
The scene of terror and of war.

As nearer still the monarch drew
(Her starry flag display'd to view),
He ask'd a Triton of his train,
"What flag was this that rode the main?

"A ship of such a gallant mien
This many a day I have not seen:
To no mean power can she belong,
So swift, so warlike, stout, and strong.

"See how she mounts the foaming wave,
Where other ships would find a grave:
Majestic, awful, and serene,
She walks the ocean like its queen."

"Great monarch of the hoary deep,
Whose trident awes the waves to sleep,"
Replied a Triton of his train,
"This ship that stems the Western main

"To those new, rising States belongs,
Who, in resentment of their wrongs,
Oppose proud Britain's tyrant sway,
And combat her by land and sea.

"This pile, of such superior fame,
From their strict union takes her name;
For them she cleaves the briny tide,
While terror marches by her side.

"When she unfurls her flowing sails,
Undaunted by the fiercest gales,
In dreadful pomp she ploughs the main,
While adverse tempests rage in vain.

"When she displays her gloomy tier,
The boldest Britons freeze with fear,
And, owning her superior might,
Seek their best safety in their flight.

"But, when she pours the dreadful blaze,
And thunder from her cannon plays,
The bursting flash that wings the ball
Compels those foes to strike or fall.

"Though she, with her triumphant train
Might fill with awe the British main,
Yet, filial to the land that bore,
She stays to guard her native shore.

"Though she might make their cruisers groan
That sail beneath the torrid zone,
She kindly lends a nearer aid,
Annoys them here, and guards the trade.

"Now traversing the Eastern main,
She greets the shores of France and Spain:
Her gallant flag, display'd to view,
Invites the Old World to the New.

"This task achieved, behold her go
To seas congeal'd with ice and snow,
To either tropic, and the line,
Where suns with endless fervor shine.

"Not, Argo, in thy womb was found
Such hearts of brass as here abound:
They for their golden fleece did fly,
These sail to vanquish tyranny."

---

## Charleston Harbor in 1776 and 1861.

(EXTRACT FROM MR. MURDOCH'S LECTURES.)

IN tracing the history of the relics, I have necessarily
confined myself to the sailor's record of glorious deeds
done in defence of our national honor.   Before taking leave
of my subject, I will tender you two striking pictures of
heroic devotion, which will speak for the heroism of the
soldier, displayed on a hundred memorable battle-fields,
embodying in their spirit the soul of chivalric daring which
pervades our army, rank and file.

When Fort Moultrie, in Charleston harbor, was invested

by the British in 1776, the flag was shot away during the fight. Sergeant Jasper leaped into the moat, seized the flag, and, climbing upon the ramparts, waved it above his head till another staff was erected. This noble act was performed during the hottest fire from the enemy's ships.

When the traitors of Charleston assailed Sumter (so nobly defended by the gallant Major Anderson), the following incident occurred. Sergeant Hart, who had served with the Major in Mexico, was sent down from New York by Mrs. Anderson with letters for her husband. The authorities at Charleston refused to let the sergeant pass to the fort unless he gave his parole not to bear arms in the defence. This was acceded to, and the faithful soldier executed his mission of love. During the fiercest bombardment of the fort, while standing, watching the flying shells and balls, from a sheltered position, the sergeant saw the old flag stricken down by a shot. Without stopping to argue on the exact extent of a non-combatant's passiveness, true to the instincts of a loyal citizen, he sprang forward, secured the Stars and Stripes, and, from the most prominent position on the works, waved them forth, until another staff was raised, and then, arranging the halliards with his own hands, ran up the starry emblem, to defy once more the murderous assault of the would-be assassins of the nation's life.

I will not venture to comment on the sublime acts of patriotic devotion, but will avail myself of the poetic fervor of Bayard Taylor to sing the praises of the soldier's deeds, and blend the spirit of 1776 and 1812 with that of '61, '62, and '63.

## Scott and the Veteran.

BY BAYARD TAYLOR.

An old and crippled veteran to the War Department came:
He sought the chief who led him on many a field of fame,—
The chief who shouted, "Forward!" where'er his banner rose,
And bore its stars in triumph behind the flying foes.

"Have you forgotten, general," the batter'd soldier cried,
"The days of eighteen hundred twelve, when I was at your
    side?
Have you forgotten Johnson, that fought at Lundy's Lane?
'Tis true I'm old and pension'd; but I want to fight again."

"Have I forgotten," said the chief, "my brave old soldier?
    No!
And here's the hand I gave you then, and let it tell you so;
But you have done your share, my friend; you're crippled, old,
    and gray,
And we have need of younger arms and fresher blood to-day."

"But, general," cried the veteran, a flush upon his brow,
"The very men who fought with us, they say, are traitors now.
They've torn the flag of Lundy's Lane, our old Red, White,
    and Blue;
And, while a drop of blood is left, I'll show that drop is true.

"I'm not so weak but I can strike, and I've a good old gun,
To get the range of traitors' hearts and pick them one by one.
Your minie rifles and such arms it a'n't worth while to try;
I couldn't get the hang of them; but I'll keep my powder
    dry!"

"God bless you, comrade!" said the chief; "God bless your
loyal heart!
But younger men are in the field, and claim to have their part:
They'll plant our sacred banner in each rebellious town,
And woe henceforth to any hand that dares to pull it down!"

"But, general," still persisting, the weeping veteran cried,
"I'm young enough to follow, so long as you're my guide;
And some, you know, must bite the dust, and that at least can I:
So give the young ones a place to fight, but me a place to die!

"If they should fire on Pickens, let the colonel in command
Put me upon the rampart, with the flag-staff in my hand:
No odds how hot the cannon smoke, or how the shells may fly,
I'll hold the Stars and Stripes aloft, and hold them till I die!

"I'm ready, general, so you let a post to me be given
Where Washington can see me, as he looks from highest
heaven,
And says to Putnam at his side, or may-be General Wayne,
'There stands old Billy Johnson, that fought at Lundy's
Lane!

"And when the fight is hottest, before the traitors fly,
When shell and ball are screeching and bursting in the sky,
If any shot should hit me, and lay me on my face,
My soul would go to Washington's and not to Arnold's place."

14*

# Paul Jones, and the Navy of the Revolution.

(EXTRACT FROM MR. MURDOCH'S LECTURES.)

IN these days of degeneracy and disloyalty, as expressed
in the rebellious South and in the sympathy the rebellion
has met with at home and abroad, it is a pleasing duty to
bring forth and review the generous acts of those men who
came from foreign countries and imperilled property and
life to aid our fathers in protecting and perpetuating the
rights of man. Foremost among these brave men stands
Paul Jones, whose noble devotion to the cause of freedom
has won for his name an imperishable record in our naval
history.

Commodore Paul Jones was born in Scotland. His father,
a respectable man in the lower walks of life, could only
afford him a moderate education for a boy twelve years old.
Having fed his roving fancy with tales of adventure gleaned
from the old sailors who frequented the ship-yards and
lounged in the nautical haunts along the shores of Solway
Frith, near his home, he resolved at that age to visit America. Circumstances favored his intentions; and here he
passed several years of his life. He became engaged in
commerce, and studied navigation. This he carried into
practical experience during two or three voyages to the
coast of Africa; and, after holding several important commands in the commercial marine, he tendered his services
to the infant navy of the Colonies,—satisfied that their
cause was the cause of justice and of right, and anxious
to distinguish himself as a defender of that which his
conscience approved and to which his generous and heroic
sympathies directed him. We first find him commanding

the Ariel, one of the two ships that constituted the navy of Congress at that time. Jones was now twenty-eight years of age. The historian claims for him the honor of raising, with his own hands, the flag of independent America on board the Ariel, in the Delaware River,—the first time it was ever displayed on board a regular American vessel of war. From the Ariel he was transferred to the Ranger, and bore in her to France despatches of the victory of Saratoga. While in a French port, he received from the French commander the first salute that was ever given to the American flag in a foreign port.

In 1778, he made a descent on the English coast, surprising a garrison and capturing a fort, destroying shipping, and taking a king's ship, called the Drake, in Carrickfergus Bay, throwing the coasts of Ireland and Scotland into consternation, and causing the British Government great expenditure in fortifying their harbors. We now approach the most daring exploit of this truly great character.

In company with a fleet of vessels fitted out in France, by the assistance of the French Government, aided by the exertions of Benjamin Franklin, we find him at sea, preying on the English commerce, and boldly attacking the ships of the enemy wherever met.

September 2, 1776, Paul Jones, in the Bonhomme Richard, in company with the Pallas and the Alliance, fell in with the returning Baltic fleet of merchantmen, under convoy of the king's ships, the Serapis, forty-four guns, and the Countess of Scarborough, twenty-two guns. These ships at once signalled the merchantmen to keep on their course, while they boldly stood out to sea, inviting an action. The battle was fought on the eastern coast of England, off Flamborough Head, at night, the moon occasionally lighting the combatants. Paul Jones, in the Bonhomme Richard, fought the Serapis, while the Pallas engaged the Scarborough. The Alliance frigate, under the command of Captain Landais, a Frenchman,—who, from his record, must have been either a madman or a traitor to the cause he had espoused,—kept aloof during the greater part of the fight, only coming in towards its close, to fire broadside after broadside in such a direction as to injure the Bonhomme Richard as much, if not more, than the enemy,—in fact, leaving it doubtful against which vessel he had aimed his guns. After a severe fight, the Scarborough struck her flag to the Pallas.

Paul Jones, who had maintained a desperate conflict with his antagonist, despairing of conquering him at long range, on account of the disabled condition of many of his guns, and of the inferior calibre of the remainder, now determined to run the Serapis aboard. This bold manœuvre was successfully accomplished, and, lashing his ship to that of his foe, he continued the fight, as sailors say, "yard-arm to yard-arm," the gunners on the lower decks of both vessels actually fighting through the port-holes to prevent one another from ramming home the charges of their guns.

Some of the lower-deck cannon on board the Richard burst in the earlier part of the action, tearing up the decks above in a frightful manner. During a momentary lull in the firing, occasioned by this accident, the British commander hailed, and demanded whether the Richard had surrendered, to which Paul Jones replied, "No: we have not yet begun to fight." Striding from point to point, the hero might then be seen, now on the deck slippery with blood, now in the shrouds, trumpet in hand, calling away his boarders to hurl them on the deck of the enemy, stimulating his crew to renewed efforts by words of fiery courage, and leading in the van of every danger.

Let us here imagine the commodore turning suddenly at a cry for quarter, uttered by some craven souls who thought the vessel was sinking. The flag-staff was shot away, the ensign was trailing in the water over the stern; voices cry from out the smoke and darkness, "Quarter, for God's sake! We are sinking!" Pistols flash, and a stentorian voice is heard shouting, "Who are those rascals? Shoot them! kill them!" The rush of hurrying feet across the deck, the dash of heavy bodies leaping through the hatchways, tell, in unmistakable terms, that the speaker there is more to be dreaded than the terrors of the sinking ship.

From all accounts, the conflict at this juncture must have been terrible beyond description. While the sides of the ship were being literally pounded to pieces by cannon actually fired within a few feet of the timbers they were crushing, the men, maddened to fury by wounds, flame, and smoke, were fighting with hatchets, pikes, and every other weapon at hand, including even the rammers of the guns; and while this was going on below the decks, the rigging and round-tops presented a still more frightful picture. The vessels were now both on fire, the flames pouring up through the gaps in the deck, licking up the tarry ropes and tackle, and throwing around all a lurid light of terror. The yard-arms of the contending ships crossed each other's decks, entangled and enveloped in smoke, crowded with sailors, cutting and hacking at each other, more like devils than men, while some exploded hand-grenades on the heads of those below. The musketry of the marines rattling from the decks and blending with the sullen roar of cannon, the sharpshooters in the tops, dealing death from above, the shouts of the commanders, the cries of the combatants, of pain or of defiance, the crackling flames shooting through enshrouding smoke, the decks all ablaze with fire or enveloped in Egyptian darkness,—these separate horrors all combined to render that midnight death-struggle on the ocean more like a picture of fiends and furies, conjured up to delight the hellish fancies of infernal spectators, realizing the words of Shakspeare, "Hell is empty, and all the devils are here."

And yet such are the scenes from which we draw our inspirations of heroism, and in which we see our cherished types of valor, daring, and patriotism.

How truly might these gallant combatants realize that fierce pleasure Sir Walter Scott speaks of,—

> "The stern joy that clansmen feel
> In foemen worthy of their steel"!

This terrible and obstinate conflict lasted three and a half hours; and when the Englishman surrendered, his vessel was found to be anchored, and the flag nailed to the mast. Some time, therefore, elapsed before the usual token of submission could be made manifest; while our vessel was only kept afloat by the almost superhuman efforts of a body of prisoners, who had been confined below decks, and had been during the latter part of the action set at liberty by the officer in charge. Had it not been for this circumstance, the Bonhomme Richard would have sunk alongside her enemy before his flag had been struck.

Thus ended one of the most sanguinary battles ever fought on the ocean. The Bonhomme Richard sank the next morning,—the officers and crew being first transferred on board the English ship, which was almost as badly disabled as the Richard. She, however, was kept afloat, but with great difficulty, and finally made the Texel, to which port Paul Jones had been ordered for repairs.

The Alliance now became the flag-ship of our hero, and in her he made another of those voyages which called forth the eulogy of the nation, and during which the enemy's gazettes had, as usual, matter enough for comment on the movements and doings of the "Bold Buccaneer," as they termed him.

During the next year, we find Commodore Jones in America once more, where he received a vote of thanks from Congress, and the appointment to the command of an American seventy-four; but, the war terminating soon after, he did not get into active service again. The King of France presented him with a gold-mounted sword, and requested Congress to decorate him with the "Order of Merit." This was done, the badge, &c. having been sent over for the purpose. Congress also presented him with a gold medal, in consideration of the zeal, prudence, and intrepidity with which he had sustained the honor of the American flag. He was now the Chevalier Paul Jones, and, having returned to Paris on a mission for the United States, he was honored by the Empress of Russia with an appointment as rear-admiral of the Russian fleet. He served with distinction, and was invested with the order of "St. Anna." He retired for the last time to Paris, and died there, much honored and respected. His funeral was marked by public ceremonies befitting a hero and a good man, which there is no doubt he was. "That Paul Jones was a remarkable man," says Cooper, the naval historian, "cannot justly be questioned. In his enterprises are to be discovered much of that boldness of conception that marks a great naval captain; though his most celebrated battle is probably the one in which he evinced no other very high quality than that of invincible resolution to conquer. The expedient of running the Serapis aboard was like him; and it was the only chance of victory that was left."

It will be remembered that the lamented Lawrence intended to accomplish the same result in the grapple with the Shannon. But accident frustrated his plan, and gave the enemy an advantage, which resulted in the capture of our ship and the death of her commander.

In all bold and daring departures from custom or orders, success throws a halo of glory around the master-spirit of innovation, while failure is attended with obloquy and . oblivion.

Frost, in his "Naval Memoirs," pays this tribute to the memory of the man the nation honored,—"It is but just to place him among the first of our naval commanders; for his splendid career exhibited a degree of courage and ability which has been surpassed by none of those who have succeeded him in the brilliant line of our naval heroes."

---

## The Bonhomme Richard.

WHEN in a French port awaiting the result of Franklin's negotiations regarding the fitting out of a naval force for the service of the Republic, Paul Jones became weary of inactivity, and what he thought procrastination on the part of the agents. Therefore he went to Paris, to urge the proceeding personally. The result was that complete success crowned his efforts. He returned to the seaboard and fitted out his vessels without further delay. To the one he had selected as his flag-ship he gave the name of The Goodman Richard. It will be remembered in Franklin's Almanac of Poor Richard there were many terse and wise proverbs and sayings, among which was one to the effect that what a man wants to accomplish well and speedily he had better attend to himself, rather than trust to the assistance of others. So Paul Jones called his ship The Goodman Richard, in compliment to the sayings of Benjamin Franklin.

The following old-fashioned nautical song was a favorite in my boyhood. I have heard my father sing it with great delight. I am not able to give the author's name. Whatever may be said of the poetry, the sentiment is truly American, while the fire of national pride burns in every line.

## Paul Jones.

AN American frigate from Baltimore came,
Her guns mounted forty, the Richard by name;
Went to cruise in the Channel of old England,
With a noble commander, Paul Jones was the man.
We had not sail'd long before we did espy
A large forty-four, and a twenty close by:
These two warlike ships, full laden with store,
Our captain pursued to the bold Yorkshire shore.

At the hour of twelve, Pierce came alongside.
With a loud speaking-trumpet. "Whence came you?" he
    cried;
"Quick give me an answer, I hail'd you before,
Or this very instant a broadside I'll pour."
Paul Jones he exclaim'd, "My bravo boys, we'll not run:
Let every brave seaman stand close to his gun;"
When a broadside was fired by these brave Englishmen,
And we bold buckskin heroes return'd it again.

We fought them five glasses, five glasses most hot,
Till fifty brave seamen lay dead on the spot,
And full seventy more lay bleeding in their gore,
Whilst Pierce's loud cannon on the Richard did roar.

Our gunner, affrighted, unto Paul Jones he came,
"Our ship is a-sinking, likewise in a flame;"
Paul Jones he replied, in the height of his pride,
"If we can do no better, we'll sink alongside."

At length our shot flew so quick, they could not stand:
The flag of proud Britain was forced to come down,
The Lion bore down and the Richard did rake,
Which caused the heart of Richard to ache.
Come now, my brave buckskin, we've taken a prize,
A large forty-four, and a twenty likewise;
They are both noble vessels, well laden with store!
We will toss off the can to our country once more.

God help the poor widows, who shortly must weep
For the loss of their husbands, now sunk in the deep!
We'll drink to brave Paul Jones, who, with sword in hand,
Shone foremost in action, and gave us command.

## Our Heroes.

BY LUCY HAMILTON HOOPER.

Gay leaders in the "German's" maze,
   Light danglers by a lady's chair,
White-gloved, soft-voiced,—your place of old
   Knows you no more. Where are you?—where?

Our lists of "dancing men" grow thin;
   And, as one turns the page, one sees
The old familiar names no more:
   They're writ on sadder lists than these

Dark records of red battle-fields,
   Of crimson sands and gory sod,
Where, 'mid the rush and roar of war,
   Brave souls and true went up to God.

We read the lists of those who pine
   In loathsome prisons far away,
And sigh to greet each well-known name:
   *There* are our carpet-knights to-day

And if, in haunts forsaken long,
   We greet once more a well-known face,
On pallid brow and faded lip
   We mark the fatal fever-trace:

Or, with full heart and eyes, we note
   The gallant soldier's empty sleeve:
Yet back, unshed, we press our tears!
   We are too proud of him to grieve!

And, gallant hearts! undaunted still
   By perill'd life and wearing pain,
They turn from loving homes away,
   Their scarce-saved lives to stake again.

Scarce has each fearful wound been heal'd,
  Scarce has the fever ceased to burn,
When from each wan lip rings the cry,
  "Our country needs us! we return!

"We go to bear her flag once more
  To victory 'neath the Southern sky.
We've suffer'd for her cause; and now
  We're ready for that cause to die!"

My country! though thy flag to-day
  Droops, dimm'd and rent by rebel guns,
Thou hast no cause to faint or fear!
  Be proud the while thou hast such sons!

THE END.

www.ingramcontent.com/pod-product-compliance
Lightning Source LLC
Chambersburg PA
CBHW030849270326
41928CB00008B/1281